Christianity has alway il government, yet as American culture faces away, es at an alarming rate, Christians are being forced to think more carefully about what the Bible says about government than they have in the recent past. In *Just Thinking: About the State*, Darrell Harrison and Virgil Walker have provided an invaluable tool to help Christians do just that. The greatest strength of this book is its reliance on the sufficiency and authority of God's Word in thinking carefully about relevant issues such as the nature of government, capitalism, abortion, politics, ethnicity, and elections. The Bible is not silent about civil government—indeed, God himself instituted it—so Darrell and Virgil wisely and pastorally guide modern Christians to think biblically about these matters in an age when so many extrabiblical ideologies battle for our attention. This is a must-read resource to help Christians discern how to live faithfully in their dual citizenship in the kingdom of God and the kingdoms of men.

—**Scott Aniol, PhD**
Associate Professor and Director of Doctoral Worship Studies | Southwestern Baptist Theological Seminary

Rooted deeply in the Scriptures, this book tackles the difficult issues for Christians to balance the role of government and their faith. It's a great resource for any believer who wants to enter such discussions with facts and not just emotions.

—**Dr. Curt Dodd**
Senior Pastor | Westside Church

Darrell and Virgil are the familiar voices on *Just Thinking*— the most popular and most influential long-form evangelical podcast in the world. They have a well-deserved reputation for careful analysis, bold clarity, biblical wisdom, and quotable phrasing. Those same qualities distinguish their writing, and that makes this book not only a joy to read but also an indispensable resource—especially in an age of increasing conflict between Christ and Caesar.

—**Phil Johnson**
Executive Director | Grace to You

The ministry that God has entrusted to me is known for engaging false doctrine and false teachers, but I have never witnessed anything so destructive that has been accepted so quickly and so uncritically by so many evangelicals as the social justice movement. It has swept into the church like wildfire and has, to varying degrees, been promoted by voices long been trusted as theologically conservative stalwarts of truth. Many Christians are confused as to how to even understand these issues, much less how to biblically engage them—understandably so. Many are afraid of being called a racist if they do not acquiesce to the prevailing cultural winds. This is why I am so profoundly grateful for *Just Thinking: About the State*. In this book, Darrell Harrison and Virgil Walker engage hot-button issues with intellectual rigor and theological precision. They pull no punches and make no apologies in diagnosing the root problems our society faces and in calling Christians to boldly stand on God's unchanging Word. I am honored to count both Darrell and Virgil as personal friends and could not be more enthusiastic in commending this tremendously helpful resource to you.

—**Justin Peters**
Justin Peters Ministries

There is not one single aspect of the Christian life for which a biblical worldview is not both necessary and practical. Every believer in Jesus Christ had better think critically, biblically, and faithfully about engagement in today's ever-changing public square. Darrell Harrison and Virgil Walker make this case abundantly clear in *Just Thinking: About the State*. It is a must-read for any serious Christian.

—**Ryan Helfenbein**
Executive Director | Standing for Freedom Center at Liberty University

In this excellent work, Darrell Harrison and Virgil Walker faithfully contend for the faith that was once for all delivered to the saints (Jude 3). As we journey onward toward our eternal home, where we will finally and forever be under the visible reign of King Jesus, we must keep our eyes fixed on Christ and exercise biblical discernment along the journey. This is the time for the church to live out the gospel in the public sphere, and Darrell Harrison and Virgil Walker point out the Christian's call while urging us to be faithful in this age of compromise.

—**Josh Buice**
Pastor | Pray's Mill Baptist Church
Founder and President | G3 Ministries

So nice, I had to read it twice! As expected, Darrell and Virgil pull no punches in *Just Thinking: About the State*. It is convicting, biblical, and at times, uncomfortably uncompromising. The church needs this book, and we need it now.

—**John L. Cooper**
Singer | Skillet
Author | *Awake and Alive to Truth*
Host | *Cooper Stuff* podcast

The unpredictable events of the past five years—and especially the last year and a half—have caused believers to give unprecedented consideration to Scripture's teaching on the Christian's relationship to government. Spheres of authority, church-state relations, the Christian's role in the political process, avoiding both escapism and transformationalism, giving to Caesar what is his and to God what is His, showing compassion without devolving into the social gospel, matters of race, justice, and church unity—it has been overwhelming! So many have had to confront these issues in more practical ways than we could have imagined.

Through this tumultuous time, over and over again I have retreated to the sound, biblical counsel of my dear brothers Darrell and Virgil. They have been God's gifts of courage and faithfulness in a season of the church's confusion, obfuscation, and mission drift—prophetic voices of reason to a church gone astray. This book represents the best of that sane, Scripture-saturated commentary that has blessed so many. How must believers bring the Bible to bear on our political views, our participation in the public square, and the hot-button social issues confronting the church today? *Just Thinking: About the State* is an invaluable resource for answering those questions. Read and be blessed.

—**Mike Riccardi, PhD**
The Master's Seminary Pastor | Local Outreach Ministries,
Grace Community Church

Darrell Harrison and Virgil Walker have served the church well in this superb foundational work as they encourage biblical thinking about the issues of government that are increasingly relevant in our day. May God use their efforts to help shape the thinking of our generation so that generations to come may benefit and Christ's kingdom may expand and advance.

—**Anthony Mathenia**
Pastor | ChristChurch

Just Thinking:
about the state

Just Thinking:
about the state

Darrell Harrison & Virgil Walker

MINISTRIES
CAPE CORAL, FLORIDA

Just Thinking: About the State

Copyright © 2021 Founders Press

All rights reserved. Written permission must be secured from the author to use or reproduce any part of this book, except for brief quotations in critical review or articles.

Unless otherwise indicated, Scripture quotations taken from the (NASB®) New American Standard Bible®, Copyright © 1960, 1971, 1977, 1995 by The Lockman Foundation. Used by permission. All rights reserved. www.lockman.org.

Scripture quotations marked NASB taken from the (NASB®) New American Standard Bible®, Copyright © 1960, 1971, 1977, 1995, 2020 by The Lockman Foundation. Used by permission. All rights reserved. www.lockman.org.

Scripture quotations marked ESV are from the ESV® Bible (The Holy Bible, English Standard Version®), copyright © 2001 by Crossway, a publishing ministry of Good News Publishers. Used by permission. All rights reserved.

Scripture quotations marked ERV are from the Easy-to-Read® Bible, copyright © 1987, 2004 Bible League International. Used by permission. All rights reserved.

Scripture quotations marked (NIV) are taken from the Holy Bible, New International Version®, NIV®. Copyright © 1973, 1978, 1984, 2011 by Biblica, Inc.® Used by permission of Zondervan. All rights reserved worldwide. www.zondervan.com The "NIV" and "New International Version" are trademarks registered in the United States Patent and Trademark Office by Biblica, Inc.®

Scripture quotations marked NRSV are from the New Revised Standard Version Bible, copyright © 1989 National Council of the Churches of Christ in the United States of America. Used by permission. All rights reserved worldwide.

Published by Founders Press
P.O. Box 150931 • Cape Coral, FL • 33915
Phone: (888) 525-1689
Electronic Mail: officeadmin@founders.org
Website: www.founders.org

Cover design by Jaye Bird LLC
Typesetting by InkSmith Editorial Services

ISBN: 978-1-943539-23-9

Dedication

To my parents, Barbara and Samuel, who exemplified for me a godly work ethic and taught me never to make excuses, regardless how adverse the situation or circumstance.

~ Darrell

To my parents, Clarence (Benny) and Mary, who taught me to keep God first, to work hard, and to never stop learning.

~ Virgil

Contents

Foreword by John MacArthur ix

Introduction by Tom Ascol 1

  1. Government 5

  2. Socialism 27

  3. Capitalism 45

  4. A Social Savior 59

  5. The Born-Alive Act 73

  6. Black Lives Matter and Abortion 89

  7. Politics and the Black Church 105

  8. Reparations 119

  9. The Equality Act 139

10. Elections 157

About the Authors 183

Scripture Index 185

Foreword

John MacArthur
Pastor | Grace Community Church, Author,
Teacher | Grace To You, Chancellor | The Master's University

> "Render to Caesar the things that are Caesar's,
> and to God the things that are God's." (Mark 12:17)

Jesus's famous statement about taxpaying recognizes that there is a legitimate role for secular civil government. Within the realm of Caesar's legal authority, believers have a duty to submit to the government even when it might be unpleasant or costly—and even if Caesar isn't particularly likeable. Christians in first-century Rome literally lived and worked in Caesar's immediate neighborhood while Nero was emperor. According to Philippians 4:22, a few believers even worked or lived in his household. Nero was one of the most notoriously cruel and thoroughly wicked rulers who ever sat on any earthly throne. But Paul's epistle to that congregation made clear that a Christian's obedience to Caesar's legitimate power is nevertheless a divine mandate. Christians are not supposed to be political insurrectionists. "Let every person be subject to the governing authorities. For there is no authority except from God, and those that exist have been instituted by God. Therefore whoever resists the authorities resists what God has appointed, and those who resist will incur judgment" (Romans 13:1–2).

At the same time, Jesus's words about rendering to Caesar also implicitly draw a clear line of demarcation between the kingdom of God and the kingdoms of this world. "The things that are God's" do not belong to Caesar. Furthermore, Christ is Lord over all (Acts 10:36), meaning he is the supreme authority in the universe, even over Caesar. So when the whims and edicts of civil government are clearly at odds with the law of God, or when Caesar tries to overrule and supplant the sovereign prerogatives of Christ, we must obey God rather than men (Acts 5:29).

A time is coming, of course, when all the kingdoms of this world will be annexed and absorbed into the eternal kingdom of Christ, and he will reign in perfect righteousness forever and ever (Revelation 11:15). In the meantime, however, there always will be tension between the two realms. Caesar, of course, wants to consolidate everything under his authority. Civil government—no matter how well intentioned it may be at the start—will eventually attempt to seize and exercise authority over "the things that are God's."

Even in a constitutional republic founded with safeguards designed to keep the government out of church doctrine and polity, Caesar relentlessly tries to encroach into "the things that are God's." The government's endless push into church affairs has never been more obvious than currently in America. Legislation is in place (and more is pending) that would hand Caesar power to regulate whom churches can employ and what they can require of staff and church members with regard to sexual purity, gender identity, abortion, the role of women, and a growing list of similar moral issues. Politicians have even proposed legislation raising the charge of "hate speech" to try to silence parts of the biblical message.

Meanwhile, government schools routinely indoctrinate children (starting in preschool) with amoral values. Government-mandated sex education purposely denigrates biblical standards and aggressively promotes the normalization of a list of sexual perversions too obscene to name in polite society. The government has made it easy for children to obtain birth control, sex-change counseling, or an abortion—all without their parents' knowledge, even while they are deemed too young to be given an aspirin from the school nurse without a parent's permission.

Mandatory government-funded programs inculcate students and employees in the doctrines of critical race theory, a pernicious and quasi-religious stew of ethnic resentment steeped in neo-Marxist ideology. Courts and legislatures throughout the Western world have actively promoted the secularization of all society. They have championed gender fluidity. They have tried to ennoble various sexual perversions. They have forced Christian shop owners out of business over matters of conscience. And they have adopted an extensive agenda of public policies that are overtly hostile to biblical values.

Governments across North America used the COVID-19 crisis to impose severe restrictions on practically every facet of Christian worship. For months on end, arbitrary and frequently changing rules limited everything from congregational singing to group prayer meetings (even in private homes). Some governors banned religious gatherings completely. In Canada, pastors were arrested and jailed—in one case for several weeks. A church where people continued to gather was forcibly closed, barricaded, and surrounded by armed guards who kept worshipers away.

But the most alarming threat to the spiritual health and liberty of the church comes not from the government and not merely from the spiraling secularization of popular culture. A danger more serious by orders of magnitude arises from within the church itself, because contemporary evangelicals have cultivated an atmosphere of blithe indifferentism in their own movement. Critical thinking and careful discernment are generally scorned within the evangelical movement today. Church leaders painstakingly study culture so they can imitate what is popular, rather than confronting the cultural drift with biblical truth. One clear example of this is the growing acceptance of critical race theory within the church. This is occurring even while careful thinkers in the secular academic world have begun pointing out that critical theory is a dangerous quasi-Marxist ideology whose completely predictable effect is to provoke deeper division and aggravate more animosity between already-adverse people groups. The only reason Christians would have for adopting the tenets of critical race theory or intersectional feminism—even as supposedly "helpful analytical tools"—is because postmodern evangelicals have a pathological craving reminiscent of the Israelites in 1 Samuel 8:20 who wanted to be like the surrounding nations.

Let's not forget that "friendship with the world is enmity with God" (James 4:4). The church must awaken to these trends and respond appropriately, resisting the temptation to fight with carnal weapons as if this were merely a bureaucratic battle or a political skirmish against flesh-and-blood enemies. It decidedly is not that. "We do not wrestle against flesh and blood, but against the rulers, against the authorities, against the cosmic powers over this present darkness, against the spiritual forces of evil in the heavenly places" (Ephesians 6:12). That speaks of unseen spiritual adversaries.

So our duty as the people of God is not to overthrow Caesar through armed insurgency. The church as a body must not abandon its true ministry as a herald of the gospel in order to become a rival political force. "The weapons of our warfare are not of the flesh" (2 Corinthians 10:4). What we are embroiled in is an ideological and spiritual conflict. And the main duty of Christ's church is to keep proclaiming the truth. That is how "we destroy arguments and every lofty opinion raised against the knowledge of God, and take every thought captive to obey Christ" (v. 5).

The whole point the apostle Paul was making when he wrote those words is that biblical truth (starting with the gospel of Jesus Christ) is the only effective weapon we have in the ongoing conflict between the kingdoms of this world and the kingdom of Christ. The truth of Scripture alone can do what no carnal warfare, no candidate, no boycott, and no partisan political party will ever accomplish. It has "divine power to destroy strongholds"—namely, those ideological prisons Caesar uses to thwart the ministry of Christ's church.

Darrell Harrison and Virgil Walker understand these things clearly. Their regular discussions on the Just Thinking podcast have established them as two of today's most thoughtful, careful, biblically anchored analysts when it comes to government policies, ideological trends, political movements, and social manias—and how such things are currently affecting the church. These are voices the church of today desperately needs to hear and heed. And this volume distills and preserves some of the best of their thinking about biblical Christianity, how we should understand the role of civil government, and how we need to respond to the ideological mess of pottage the church has all but traded its birthright for.

As every listener to their podcasts knows, Darrell and Virgil do their homework. As you might expect, their writing—like the podcast—is full of rich insight, biblical understanding, and practical help regarding tricky and often misunderstood issues. My sincere hope is that this volume will turn out to be just the first of a long series.

John MacArthur

Acknowledgments

From Darrell: My sincere thanks and appreciation to John MacArthur, Phil Johnson, Jay Flowers, and Jeremiah Johnson for providing me with godly wisdom and counsel over the course of this project, and to my wife, Melissa—my very own Katharina von Bora—who joyfully encouraged and supported me every step of the way.

From Virgil: My sincere thanks and appreciation to my wife, Tomeka; your support always begins with prayer. Thanks to our three children, who still believe their dad is cool despite his nerdiness. Thanks to Dawain Atkinson for his visionary action. I'll never forget it, brother.

Introduction

Tom Ascol
Pastor | Grace Baptist Church
President | Founders Ministries and The Institute of Public Theology

The Puritan John Flavel rightly noted that "the Providence of God is like Hebrew words—it can be read only backwards." That is because God is always doing more in any one moment or season than we can fully appreciate. Only later, as we look back, can we begin to appreciate some of the depth and breadth of His gracious work on behalf of His people during those moments that have long since passed.

That is how I think about this book by Darrell Harrison and Virgil Walker. Who could have imagined all that God was doing when Dawain Atkinson convinced them to team up for a podcast that would make *Just Thinking* an almost household brand among conservative evangelicals? Their serious, thoughtful, and biblical engagement with topics ranging from "whiteness," Black Lives Matter, and racial reconciliation to biblical unity, assurance of salvation, and worldliness in the church has captivated the minds of believers and unbelievers who, like the two of them, want to be challenged to just think for themselves.

Another strand of God's providence involves my own friendship with Darrell and Virgil. I can say that I knew them before their podcast began, but just barely. I learned of Darrell from the articles he posted on his blog, which led me to reach out to him by phone in hopes of encouraging him but with the result of being on the receiving end of great encouragement. Virgil and I had mutual friends, so we had "almost" known each other for a while. I knew about him for a year or so before I actually got to know him.

Becoming acquainted with these two faithful men and developing a friendship with them both has been one of God's great blessings to me in this latter stage of my life. Some people are easier to love at a distance than up close. That is not true of Darrell and Virgil. They "wear well." That is, the more you know them, the more you come to appreciate and love them. Their humble devotion to Christ, submission to Scripture, deep fear of God, and refusal to fear people combine to make them profitable teachers and helpful guides for anyone who wants to know the Lord better and grow in the understanding and application of His Word.

Those who are familiar with their *Just Thinking* podcast already know this about Darrell and Virgil. Those who have picked up this book are about to learn that these things are indeed so. The authors have thought deeply and taught repeatedly on issues related to God and government and Christians' responsibilities to civil authorities. In the chapters that follow, they invite readers to join them in *Just Thinking: About the State*.

Here, Darrell and Virgil have taken some issues they have addressed over the last few years in their podcast and written about them in the same bold, crisp ways they've discussed them for their listeners. They neither cut corners nor smooth rough edges off the truth. *Unvarnished* is an adjective that kept coming to mind as I read through these pages. The authors intentionally don't do nuance.

Neither do they shy away from volatile subjects, as the chapter titles alone demonstrate. Where else will you find biblical treatments of "Socialism," "A Social Savior," "The Born Alive Act," "Black Lives Matter and Abortion," "Politics and the Black Church," and "Reparations" in one book? Where the fainthearted fear to tread, Darrell and Virgil march boldly, Bibles open, with full confidence that no subject is exempt from evaluation by rigorous study of God's written Word.

Introduction

For example, in a day when more and more progressive—including many formerly conservative—Christian leaders are flirting with socialistic economic theories, Darrell and Virgil leave no doubt about their own evaluation when they say, in chapter 2 (p.42), "Socialism is a lie. It is a mirage. It is an ideology that collapses on itself because it is built on the contradiction that under the guise of morality, the pursuit of a more fair and equitable society, it is permissible to act immorally, to steal from one group of people to enrich another."

That type of bracing plain-spokenness characterizes this book. In a day of rampant moral equivocation, the authors unapologetically chart a different course. You may not always agree with what they write, but you will have no difficulty in understanding where they stand. In other words, they let their yes be yes and their no be no.

Modern Christianity needs more of this type of direct, unequivocal communication as we navigate the contemporary challenges that face us. That is especially true in the brave new world of twenty-first-century America where godlessness is codified and immorality is celebrated by a growing number of civil authorities. How are Christians to respond? What should we do?

Well, before we do anything, we should think. And our thinking should be deeply informed and shaped by the Word of God. This book is helpful in precisely this way. It not only invokes Scripture but expounds it in order to address critical matters confronting us today as a result of unwise and sometimes tyrannical civil magistrates. By writing as they do and addressing topics related to civil government that are pressing in on God's people, Darrell and Virgil not only provide helpful insights but also give us a model for thinking about any subject.

There are at least two ways their example in this book can serve Christians well as we follow them as they follow Christ. First, their approach to every topic they address reminds us that we are to "destroy arguments and every lofty opinion raised against the knowledge of God, and take every thought captive to obey Christ" (2 Corinthians 10:5 ESV). Again, you may not agree with all their understandings and applications of Scripture in this book, but you will do well to follow their example in learning to bring every matter into the light of biblical teaching.

The second way Darrell and Virgil are examples to thinking Christians today is the courage they display in holding firm to the teaching of God's Word in those areas where it is extremely unpopular. In fact, simply to assert what Scripture says on certain ethical and moral issues today is to invoke the wrath of leftists. The authors have experienced this even from so-called fellow Christians. They don't talk about it much and certainly don't dwell on it (you will see a passing reference to it in chapter 7, "Politics and the Black Church"), but I am aware of some of the castigation both men have experienced because of their unwavering commitment to the truth of Scripture. Undaunted, they keep pressing on, commending God's Word. In the process, they remind God's people of our Savior's words in Matthew 5:11–12, "Blessed are you when others revile you and persecute you and utter all kinds of evil against you falsely on my account. Rejoice and be glad, for your reward is great in heaven, for so they persecuted the prophets who were before you" (ESV).

So, read this book and be encouraged, challenged, and instructed in the ways of Jesus Christ by two of His choicest servants. As you do, pray that the Lord will help you to think carefully and biblically about the governmental authorities He has placed over us.

Tom Ascol

Cape Coral, FL

January 29, 2021

Government

On March 22, 2019, Veronique de Rugy, senior research fellow at the Mercatus Center at George Mason University, published an article on the American Institute for Economic Research website titled "France Is the Socialist Future We Should Dread."[1] In her article, de Rugy contrasts the French model of socialism with that of Cuba and Sweden and says the following regarding the detrimental realities of harboring a paternalistic view of the role of government in society:

> France was once a role model for what big government can do for its people. But it has become an embarrassing example since "The Gilets Jaunes" (French for "yellow vests") took to the streets to demonstrate against the insane amount of taxes they pay. These guys aren't upper class. They are the people who have until now supported the policies that are inevitable when you have the government providing so many services and involved so deeply in so much of the economy.
>
> The Organization for Economic Cooperation and Development (OECD) released its annual Revenue Statistics report this week,

---

[1] Veronique de Rugy, "France Is the Socialist Future We Should Dread," American Institute for Economic Research, March 22, 2019, https://www.aier.org/article/france-is-the-socialist-future-we-should-dread.

and France topped the charts, with a tax take equal to 46.2% of GDP in 2017. That's more than Denmark (46%), Sweden (44%) and Germany (37.5%), and far more than the OECD average (34.2%) or the U.S. (27.1%, which includes all levels of government).

France doesn't collect that revenue in the ways you might think.

Despite the stereotype of heavy European income taxes on the rich, Paris relies disproportionately on social-insurance, payroll and property taxes. Social taxes account for 37% of French revenue; the OECD average is 26%. Payroll and property taxes contribute 3% and 9%, compared to the OECD averages of 1% and 6%.

As a reminder, the payroll tax is very regressive; it consumes a larger share of low-and middle-class earners than rich people. In addition: then Europe adds a regressive consumption tax, the value-added tax. In France, VAT and other consumption taxes make up 24% of revenue, and that's on the low side compared to an OECD average of 33%. Consumption taxes often fall hardest on the poor and middle class, who devote a greater proportion of their income to consumption.

To be sure, the spending is also more regressive in France in that the biggest share goes to the middle and low-income earners. But it is a stupid system in which you tax one group to redistribute to that same group.

Add one more increase to an already high (and regressive) gas tax in France to the existing 214 taxes and duties and the people went nuts. They have been protesting continuously since November 17th, 2018. I don't condone the violence, but I understand why the protestors are so furious.

What Veronique de Rugy has to say is critical to helping us understand the truth about what a socialist government looks like. What is happening in France as its citizens embrace a socialist model of government is beginning to happen in America as well, particularly among the vast numbers of young people who are lining up to support political candidates who hold the same vision of regressive and redistributive government.

Not only is that vision of the role of government being embraced to an increasing degree in America *as a nation* (as evidenced, for example, by the fact that in the 2020 presidential election, at least one candidate was described as a "Democratic Socialist"[2]), it is also being embraced within certain elements of the evangelical church.

An Evangelical Issue

A case in point is what is known as the Poor People's Campaign: A National Call for Moral Revival. The campaign is led by the Rev. Dr. William J. Barber II, one of the leading evangelical social justicians in protestant evangelicalism today.[3]

In April 2018, the Poor People's Campaign produced a white paper titled "The Souls of Poor Folk: Auditing America 50 Years after the Poor People's Campaign Challenged Racism, Poverty, the War Economy/Militarism, and Our National Morality." This report contains three "mission statements," the first of which was originally put forth in 1968 by an organization known as the Committee of 100 and titled "Statements of Demands for Rights of the Poor":

> We come to you as representatives of Black, Indian, Mexican-American, Puerto-Rican, and white-Americans who are the too long forgotten, hungry and jobless outcasts in this land of plenty. We come because poor fathers and mothers want a house to live in that will protect their children against the bitter winter cold, the searing heat of summer and the rain that now too often comes in through the cracks in our roofs and walls. We have come here to say to you that we don't think it's too much to ask for a decent place to live in at reasonable prices in a country with a gross national product of 800 billion dollars. We don't think it's too radical to want to help choose the type of housing and the location. We don't think it's asking for pie in the sky to want to live in neighborhoods where our families can live and grow up

---

[2] Adrian Carrasquillo, "Democratic Socialists Will Have a Presidential Candidate in November," *Newsweek*, June 24, 2020, https://www.newsweek.com/democratic-socialists-will-have-presidential-candidate-november-1513117.
[3] "Social justicians" is our designation for those who are proponents of the modern "social justice" movement.

with dignity, surrounded by the kind of facilities and services that other Americans take for granted.[4]

It is critical to note the antecedent of the pronoun "you" that appears in the very first sentence of that mission statement. The "you" to whom the above entreaty is directed is the United States government. In fact, when you stop and reflect on the wording of the statement from the Committee of 100, it sounds a lot like a prayer. Three times in the statement the phrase "we come to you" (or "we have come to you") is used as an introduction to the petitions the writers are adjuring the federal government to answer. But the way the statement is written, it is almost as if they were addressing their petitions to God.

Consider the government-targeted supplications of the Committee of 100 with what the Word of God says about our needs and how they are supplied—and by whom:

- "And my God will supply all your needs according to His riches in glory in Christ Jesus" (Philippians 4:19).

- "But if God so clothes the grass of the field, which is alive today and tomorrow is thrown into the furnace, will He not much more clothe you? You of little faith! Do not worry then, saying, 'What will we eat?' or 'What will we drink?' or 'What are we to wear for clothing?' For the Gentiles eagerly seek all these things; for your heavenly Father knows that you need all these things. But seek first His kingdom and His righteousness, and all these things will be added to you" (Matthew 6:30–33).

- "Our help is in the name of the LORD, who made heaven and earth" (Psalm 124:8).

- "The young lions do without and suffer hunger; but they who seek the LORD will not lack any good thing" (Psalm 34:10).

---

4   Sarah Anderson et al., "The Souls of Poor Folk: Auditing America 50 Years after the Poor People's Campaign Challenged Racism, Poverty, the War Economy/Militarism, and Our National Morality," The Poor People's Campaign (Washington, DC: Institute for Policy Studies, 2018), https://www.poorpeoplescampaign.org/wp-content/uploads/2019/12/PPC-Audit-Full-410835a.pdf, 2.

- "For the Lord God is a sun and shield; the Lord gives grace and glory; He withholds no good thing from those who walk uprightly" (Psalm 84:11).
- "I will raise my eyes to the mountains; from where will my help come? My help comes from the Lord, who made heaven and earth. He will not allow your foot to slip; He who watches over you will not slumber. Behold, He who watches over Israel will neither slumber nor sleep. The Lord is your protector; the Lord is your shade on your right hand. The sun will not beat down on you by day, nor the moon by night. The Lord will protect you from all evil; He will keep your soul. The Lord will guard your going out and your coming in from this time forth and forever" (Psalm 121).

These wonderful promises of God do not negate a governmental role in society. Not at all. The question we're dealing with is this: What is the proper or, more accurately, the *biblical* role of government in society?

The French Example

We began this chapter by referencing Veronique de Rugy's analysis of French socialism. The history of that movement forms an important background to a discussion of the biblical role of government.

In 1789, the National Constituency Assembly of France adopted the Declaration of the Rights of Man and Citizen. This document was originally drafted by Marie-Joseph Paul Yves Roch Gilbert du Motier, better known as the Marquis de Lafayette.

One of the interesting things about the Declaration of the Rights of Man and Citizen is that it was closely modeled after the United States' Declaration of Independence. The close adherence to the American document was no accident. It was none other than Thomas Jefferson himself, the chief architect of the Declaration of Independence, who helped Lafayette construct the Declaration of the Rights of Man and Citizen.

In *Heaven on Earth: The Rise, Fall, and Afterlife of Socialism*, author Joshua Muravchik helps put into context the broader conversation of the role of government and the importance of Christians' developing and applying a biblical worldview of that role, particularly as that biblical worldview is contrasted against a socialist paradigm of government. Muravchik writes,

> The 1789 Declaration of the Rights of Man and Citizen tracked the U.S. Declaration of Independence in proclaiming that the reason for government was to secure men's rights. And its designation of those rights—"liberty, property, security"—resembled the American triad of "life, liberty, and the pursuit of happiness."
>
> However, as the [French] Revolution unfolded and new constitutions were written, the French added a fourth substantive right: equality. To be sure, the Americans had proclaimed that men were "created equal," but this was not a statement of policy; it was a postulate about the nature of man and his relation to God. The French innovation was to include "equality" among the essential purposes of government.
>
> The impetus behind this was not hard to understand. Whereas the core issue for the Americans in 1776 was political legitimacy, for the French in 1789 it was social status. . . . It was only in the dying days of the Revolution that someone came forward to argue there was a contradiction within the revolutionary agenda—that fulfilling the promise of equality would require not merely the abolition of feudal titles and privileges, but the institution of a new way of economic life in which individual ownership would be abolished and each citizen would be furnished with an identical portion of nature's bounty.[5]

What Muravchik is articulating is that what France did with its Declaration of the Rights of Man and Citizen is take a universal truth—and by "universal," we mean a principle or rule that applies impartially to every image-bearer of God—and genuflect to it in such a way as to turn an objective truth into a subjective one.

---

5 Joshua Muravchik, *Heaven on Earth : The Rise, Fall, and Afterlife of Socialism* (New York: Encounter, 2019), 4.

Muravchik outlined what many people, including many professing Christians, fail to understand: that there is a fundamental difference between being *created equal* and being guaranteed *equality*. The former idea is *objectively* true (Genesis 1:27; 5:2), whereas the latter concept, that each person, as stated in the French Declaration of the Rights of Man and Citizen, should be furnished by the government an "identical portion of nature's bounty," is fundamentally unbiblical.

This philosophical shift from viewing individuals as "created equal" to guaranteeing "equality" changed the societal landscape for France as it introduced to its citizens a man-centered concept of the role of government that was wholly antithetical to its God-ordained role (see Romans 13). Consequently, today, more than 230 years after the adoption of the Declaration of the Rights of Man and Citizen, France is regarded by many as a socialist country.

The French Connection

We mentioned previously that there were three mission statements presented in the white paper published by the Poor People's Campaign. The first, put forth by the Committee of 100 in 1968, was a plea to the government to meet people's material needs. The second of the two statements was authored in 2018 by the Rev. Dr. William J. Barber II:

> With the realities of systemic racism, systemic poverty, ecological devastation, the war economy and the often false moral narrative of Christian nationalism, we are in a moment in time which we need a deeply moral, deeply constitutional, anti-racist, anti-poverty, pro-labor, transformative fusion coalition where people of all different races, colors, and creeds come together and work together to engage in moral direct action, massive voter mobilization, and power building from the bottom up, state by state and even in the U.S. Capitol. We need this to change the narrative and insist that we will no longer engage in attention violence against the poor and other interlocking injustices that connect to poverty.[6]

---

6 Anderson et al., "The Souls of Poor Folk," 3.

Evident in Barber's statement is the unmistakable aroma of an ideological porridge composed of a dash of liberation theology, a smidge of socialism, and a pinch of Marxism. But that kind of philosophical concoction is precisely what you get when you've been convinced a government exists to guarantee people equal*ity* in terms of equal outcomes, as opposed to ensuring that everyone is treated equally without regard to circumstances or outcomes.

The third and final mission statement of the Poor People's Campaign is similar to the first two but was written by the Rev. Dr. Liz Theoharris, co-chair of the Poor People's Campaign. Dr. Theoharris writes, "Immigrants, Muslims, homeless people, and youth are under attack. The poor are facing severe cuts to basic social services. Millions of people are living without clean water and sanitation services. Voting rights are being suppressed and wars are being waged across the world and intensifying. These and many other crises mean it is urgent we build a poor people's campaign today."[7]

Considered together, these statements from the Committee of 100, the Rev. Dr. Barber, and the Rev. Dr. Theoharris are directly related to the development of French socialism. They represent the fruit of a worldview that concurs ideologically with the French Declaration of the Rights of Man and Citizen, which views equal*ity* as "an essential purpose of government."

The Problem of Partiality

But here's the problem: you cannot have equality without engaging in partiality. And in Scripture, partiality is sin. Consider what the following verses teach about partiality:

- "You shall not do injustice in judgment; you shall not show partiality to the poor nor give preference to the great, but you are to judge your neighbor fairly" (Leviticus 19:15 NASB).
- "For the LORD your God is the God of gods and the Lord of lords, the great, the mighty, and the awesome God who does not show partiality nor take a bribe" (Deuteronomy 10:17).

---

7 Anderson et al., 3.

- "For there is no partiality with God" (Romans 2:11).
- "And the spies questioned [Jesus], saying, 'Teacher, we know that You speak and teach correctly, and You are not partial to anyone, but You teach the way of God on the basis of truth'" (Luke 20:21 NASB).
- "Opening his mouth, Peter said: 'I most certainly understand now that God is not one to show partiality, but in every nation the one who fears Him and does what is right is acceptable to Him'" (Acts 10:34–35 NASB).
- "If, however, you are fulfilling the royal law according to the Scripture, 'You shall love your neighbor as yourself,' you are doing well. But if you show partiality, you are committing sin and are convicted by the Law as violators" (James 2:8–9 NASB).

James 2:8 contains an important phrase we don't want you to miss: "according to the Scripture." What is the proper role of government according to the Scripture? In other words, what do the Scriptures say? What does the Word of God teach us about the role of government and its authority to confiscate and redistribute the wealth of others under the guise of creating a society of equality?

God's Sovereignty

When you reflect objectively on the three mission statements from the Poor People's Campaign, you'll notice at least four themes those statements have in common:

1. The emphasis on the poor as defined by a lack or absence of certain material possessions
2. The emphasis on material possessions as the sole remedy to material poverty
3. The emphasis on government as the sole provider of that remedy
4. The absence of any reference to God and his sovereignty in allowing such situations of material poverty to exist

Let's expand on point number four for just a moment. In Deuteronomy 8, Moses charges the Israelites after their forty years in the wilderness,

> You shall remember all the way which the LORD your God has led you in the wilderness these forty years, in order to humble you, putting you to the test, to know what was in your heart, whether you would keep His commandments or not. And He humbled you and let you go hungry, and fed you with the manna which you did not know, nor did your fathers know, in order to make you understand that man shall not live on bread alone, but man shall live on everything that comes out of the mouth of the LORD. (Deuteronomy 8:2–3)

Verse 3 says that God humbled the Israelites and "let" them be hungry. The Hebrew verb phrase "let you be hungry" literally means that God allowed their stomachs to be empty. The four common themes from the Poor People's Campaign's various mission statements bring to mind the words of C. H. Spurgeon, who, in a sermon titled "The Happy Beggar," wrote,

> There is no crime and there is no credit in being poor. Everything depends upon the occasion of the poverty. Some men are poor and are greatly to be pitied, for their poverty has come upon them without any fault of their own. God has been pleased to lay this burden upon them, and therefore they may expect to experience divine help, and ought to be tenderly considered by their brethren in Christ. Occasionally, poverty has been the result of integrity or religion, and here the poor man is to be admired or honored. At the same time, it will be observed, by all who watch with an impartial eye, that very much of the poverty about us is the direct result of idleness, intemperance, improvidence, and sin. There would probably not be one-tenth of the poverty there now is upon the face of the earth if the drinking shops were less frequented, if debauchery were less common, if idleness were banished, and extravagance abandoned.[8]

Now, given the hypersensitive milieu in which we live today, there is absolutely no doubt that many would judge those words from

---

8 Charles Haddon Spurgeon, "The Happy Beggar" (Sermon 3040, delivered May 16, 1907), Spurgeon Gems, accessed June 11, 2021, https://www.spurgeongems.org/sermon/chs3040.pdf.

Spurgeon to be uncaring, unloving, and un-Christlike in their tone, while completely disregarding the veracity and accuracy of what he said. Nevertheless, Spurgeon is absolutely correct.

Notwithstanding that God is sovereign over everything that occurs in the world (Psalm 103:19), the fact remains that the principle of reaping and sowing is not rendered moot or impotent simply because someone is materially poor (2 Thessalonians 3:10). Remember, God shows no partiality—none—to anyone, regardless of their socioeconomic situation or circumstance. Matthew 5:45 says that the Lord "causes His sun to rise on the evil and the good, and sends rain on the righteous and the unrighteous." The principle of reaping and sowing applies universally to every individual. That fact is clearly laid out by the apostle Paul in Galatians 6:7: "Do not be deceived, God is not mocked; for whatever a man sows, this he will also reap."

A God of Consequences

A primary reason why so many professing Christians today have such a misguided concept of the role of government in society is that they've completely lost sight of the fact that God is a God of consequences. The first evidence of that reality is in Genesis 2:16–17: "The Lord God commanded the man, saying, 'From any tree of the garden you may eat freely; but from the tree of the knowledge of good and evil you shall not eat, for in the day that you eat from it you will surely die.'" God made it clear to Adam that there would be consequences if he disobeyed and that those consequences would be severe—so severe, in fact, that they continue to reverberate throughout Adam's progeny to this very day.

The reason we're placing so much emphasis on this matter of consequences is that many people believe it is the role of government to come to the rescue of individuals who have violated God's precepts and principles and, as a result, are now experiencing the consequences of their disobedience. For example, countless individuals have incurred burdensome student loan debts in pursuit of a college education. And now, because they don't want to have to pay those loans back, they are placing their hopes in political candidates who have promised to have those debts canceled. But Scripture teaches that we should repay all our debts, regardless of how much we may owe.

In Romans 13:8, the apostle Paul exhorts us to "owe nothing to anyone except to love one another." Consider also Psalm 15:4, which says that God honors the person who "swears to his own hurt and does not change." In other words, God honors those who keep their word, who keep their promises, who do whatever is necessary to follow through on their obligations and commitments, whether financial or otherwise, even if doing so would be to their own detriment and injury.

Proverbs 12:22 says, "Lying lips are an abomination to the LORD, but those who deal faithfully are His delight." One way that followers of Jesus Christ can "deal faithfully" with one another is paying our debts. If you profess to be a Christian and you owe student loans, God expects you to pay those loans back. Why? Because to place that burden on the government is to cause other individuals who had nothing to do with your incurring those debts to bear the burden of your unwise decisions, and that is sin. Additionally, the question must be asked, From where—or more accurately, from *whom*—do those people think the government will get the money it needs to cancel their student loan debts in the first place? The answer: from taxpayers just like each of us, and that's simply another form of stealing.

Created Equal vs. Guaranteed Equality

A distinction must be made between the concept of *being created equal* and the idea of *guaranteed equality*. The former is biblical and objective; the latter is unbiblical and subjective.

Nowhere in Scripture is government said to be either responsible for or obligated to ensure equality of outcomes for anyone. Wayne Grudem understands this, as he explains in his book *Politics According to the Bible*: "I cannot find any justification in Scripture for thinking that government, as a matter of policy, should attempt to take from the rich and give to the poor. I do not think that government has the responsibility or the right to attempt to equalize the differences between rich and poor in a society. When it attempts to do so, significant harm is done to the economy and to the society."[9]

Taking from the "haves" and redistributing their possessions to the "have-nots" is what the Bible calls stealing. In fact, God said in Leviticus 19:15 that we are to be partial neither to the poor nor to the great. You read that correctly. It is a sin to be partial to the poor. That someone is materially poor is no excuse for the government to confiscate through coercion or force of law the possessions and property that rightfully belong to someone else.

Consider the events of Exodus 35 and 36. Moses has been commanded by God to take up an offering from among the people to construct a tabernacle. In those chapters, a significant theme is often repeated. Read carefully the following passages from those chapters, and see if you can detect what that theme is:

- "Take from among you a contribution to the LORD; whoever is of a willing heart, let him bring it as the LORD'S contribution: gold, silver, and bronze" (Exodus 35:5).
- "Everyone whose heart stirred him and everyone whose spirit moved him came and brought the LORD'S contribution for the work of the tent of meeting and for all its service and for the holy garments. Then all those whose hearts moved them, both men and women, came and brought brooches and earrings and signet rings and bracelets, all articles of gold, so did every man who presented an offering of gold to the LORD" (Exodus 35:21–22).
- "All the women whose heart stirred with a skill spun the goats' hair" (Exodus 35:26).
- "The Israelites, all the men and women, whose heart moved them to bring material for all the work, which the LORD had commanded through Moses to be done, brought a freewill offering to the LORD" (Exodus 35:29).

---

9 Wayne Grudem, *Politics According to the Bible: A Comprehensive Resource for Understanding Modern Political Issues in Light of Scripture* (Grand Rapids: Zondervan, 2010), 281.

- "Then Moses called Bezalel and Oholiab and every skillful person in whom the Lord had put skill, everyone whose heart stirred him, to come to the work to perform it" (Exodus 36:2).

Did you catch the references to "a willing heart," "heart stirred," and "freewill offering"? God wants His people to give out of compassion, not coercion.

We see another example in Matthew 19, the account of Jesus and the wealthy young ruler. The story is familiar, and in verse 21 of that chapter, Jesus says to the young man, "If you wish to be complete, go and sell your possessions and give to the poor, and you will have treasure in heaven." What is remarkable is that there are professing Christians out there today who would dare to use this verse to argue that Jesus was a socialist.

Now, notwithstanding the utter absurdity of such an assertion, let's consider thoughtfully what Jesus said to this young man. Jesus said, "Go and sell your possessions." Socialist Jesus would never have said such a thing as "sell *your* possessions," because socialist Jesus would not have acknowledged that the young man's possessions belonged to him in the first place. Socialism, by definition, does not recognize individual private property. Those possessions would have belonged to the collective, not the individual.

Additionally, socialist Jesus would never have told the young ruler to "go and *sell* your possessions." Instead, he would have commanded him to go and *give* his possessions to the poor, which, consequently, would have made the rich man poor as well (which is the ultimate result of socialism—it makes everyone equally poor). However, this giving of wealth from the rich to the poor is exactly what some believe is moral and what the government should mandate. They have confused ensuring equality with treating everyone as equal image-bearers of God. In terms of what Scripture teaches, however, "equal" is not tantamount to "equality."

Christians who hold to a paternalistic view of government do not understand how God designed government to function and operate.

The great Reformer John Calvin speaks to that in his *Institutes of the Christian Religion*, in the chapter entitled "Civil Government": "For [government] is not merely concerned with what people eat and drink and with how life is sustained, although it includes all those things by allowing men to live together . . . that each person keeps what is his and that men live together without injury or dishonesty; in short, that among Christians there should be an open expression of religion, and that in society humanity should prevail."[10] Calvin is articulating what a biblical view of government looks like: one that treats each of its citizens equally without getting involved in the business of guaranteeing equality, which invariably leads to partiality.

But consider these words in Deuteronomy 16:19, where God says, "You shall not distort justice; you shall not be partial, and you shall not take a bribe, for a bribe blinds the eyes of the wise and perverts the words of the righteous." God views it as an injustice to be partial to the poor as well as to the wealthy. The Hebrew word "partial" in Deuteronomy 16:19 literally means that we are not to notice, regard, observe, pay attention to, recognize, acknowledge, or make any type of distinction that would result in our having a sinful bias or prejudice either for or against someone.

The Role of the Church

God has laid the responsibility of caring for the poor upon the church, not the government. But even that comes with a caveat. For example, consider these verses in 1 Timothy 5 regarding widows:

- "Honor widows who are widows indeed" (v. 3).
- "Now she who is a widow indeed and who has been left alone, has fixed her hope on God and continues in entreaties and prayers night and day" (v. 5).
- "If any woman who is a believer has dependent widows, she must assist them and the church must not be burdened, so that [the church] may assist those who are widows indeed" (v. 16).

---

10 John Calvin, *Institutes of the Christian Religion*, trans. Robert White (Edinburgh, Scotland: Banner of Truth, 2014), 4.20.2.

The Greek adverb "indeed" in those verses denotes that which is a reality, as opposed to that which is pretended or conjectural. In other words, in the same way that the church is obligated to help the poor, those who would claim to be poor have a responsibility to demonstrate that they are truly in need. You can't just say you need this or that and expect the church to come to your aid. No, you must indeed be in need, according to Scripture.

Another Scriptural caveat regarding the church meeting the needs of others is found in Galatians 6:10, where Paul writes, "So then, while we have opportunity, let us do good to all people, and especially to those who are of the household of the faith." As the church works in society to meet the legitimate needs of others, it should first seek to meet the needs of those who are within the church, the "household of the faith," and then work outwardly from there.

The Government Is Not Sufficient

Contrary to what many people, including many Christians, believe, it is not the role of government to bring about equality in society. That governments should be engaged in the pursuit of social equality or social status, as was the goal of the Declaration of the Rights of Man and Citizen, particularly in terms of ensuring the distribution and ownership of certain material possessions, is never mandated in Scripture. The fact is, the real cause of all poverty in this world, whether material or otherwise, is sin, and sin is something that no government has the power to rescue us from. As the apostle Paul writes in Romans 8:19–21, "For the anxious longing of the creation waits eagerly for the revealing of the sons of God. For the creation was subjected to futility, not willingly, but because of Him who subjected it, in hope that the creation itself also will be set free from its slavery to corruption into the freedom of the glory of the children of God."

No government on earth has the power to set this world free from its slavery to the corruption in which it has existed since Eve and Adam sinned in garden of Eden. And yet that is how many people today view government. They see it as being inherently endowed with the power and authority to create a world wherein all our needs—and many of our *wants*—are met. They look to the government to create a world devoid of consequences and accountability where they can live lives of complete autonomy apart from God.

A key driver for that kind of mindset (even to the comparatively small degree it currently exists within the church) is that the church is full of people who are discontented with their lives. They want a life of comfort, ease, and convenience. They're not satisfied with what Paul says in 1 Timothy 6:8, that "if we have food and covering, with these we shall be content."

Instead of praying as Jesus taught in what is commonly referred to as the Lord's Prayer, "Give us this day our daily bread," they not only want the bread, they want the mayonnaise, the mustard, the lettuce, the tomato, the pickles, the onions, and the choicest, finely sliced deli meat. They want the whole sandwich served to them on a platter. And if they can't get the kind of meal they want from God, they'll just get it from the government.

But the kind of bread Jesus offers the world is the bread that leads to eternal life, not mere temporal satisfaction—which is the most any government can promise to provide its citizens. Consider Christ's words in John 6:33–34: "'For the bread of God is that which comes down out of heaven, and gives life to the world.' Then they said to Him, 'Lord, always gives us this bread.'"

"Lord, always give us this bread"—is that your prayer today? Is that the cry of your heart—"Lord, always give me the bread that gives life to the world?" In other words, "Lord, always give me You." Jesus Christ, the Bread of Life, knows your every need and is sufficient to meet that need in and of himself. That is why Jesus said in John 6:27, "Do not work for the food which perishes, but for the food which endures to eternal life."

The French economist of the mid-nineteenth century, Frédéric Bastiat, said,

> Self-preservation and self-development are common aspirations among all people. And if everyone enjoyed the unrestricted use of his faculties and the free disposition of the fruits of his labor,

social progress would be ceaseless, uninterrupted, and unfailing. But there is also another tendency that is common among people. When they can, they wish to live and prosper at the expense of others. This is no rash accusation. Nor does it come from a gloomy and uncharitable spirit. The annals of history bear witness to the truth of it: the incessant wars, mass migrations, religious persecutions, universal slavery, dishonesty in commerce, and monopolies. This fatal desire has its origin in the very nature of man—in that primitive, universal, and insuppressible instinct that impels him to satisfy his desires with the least possible pain.[11]

The Christian understands that there will be pain in this life, and that true lasting happiness will never be a reality in this sinful world (Romans 8:18-21). The kind of happiness the church anticipates is one that no government can provide. As the Scripture declares in 2 Peter 3:13, "But according to His promise we are looking for new heavens and a new earth, in which righteousness dwells."

Only God Provides What We Really Need

Yes, there is a role for government to play in society, but that role is not to provide cradle-to-grave security in a world that is passing away (1 John 2:15–17). Paul writes in Romans 13:4 that the governing authorities are to act as ministers of God to us for our good. Paul does not say that the government *is God*. God alone is the One who meets our every need. Paul, in speaking of God in Romans 8:32, says that "He who did not spare His own Son, but delivered Him over for us all, how will He not also with Him freely give us all things?"

And as C. H. Spurgeon said, "In his Church, Christ teaches us that, if we have more than others, we simply hold it in trust for those who have less than we have; and I believe that some of the Lord's children are poor in order that there may be an opportunity for their fellow-Christians to minister to them out of their abundance."[12]

---

[11] Frederic Bastiat, *The Law*, trans. Dean Russell (Irvington-on-Hudson, NY: Foundation for Economic Education, 1998),5–6.
[12] Charles Spurgeon, "Poverty," Exploring the Mind and Heart of the Prince of Preachers, accessed June 11, 2021, http://www.spurgeon.us/mind_and_heart/quotes.

In contrast to the Poor People's Campaign, whose mission statements are saturated with entreaties to the government for redress of their collectivist concerns, Jesus Christ said in Matthew 11:28: "Come to Me, all who are weary and heavy-laden, and I will give you rest."

In this sin-sick world in which we live, none of us will ever have all our needs met. Another way of saying that is that God never promised us equality in this life. In fact, not even in the new earth will there be equality, as each person will be rewarded based on the deeds he or she has done. We know this from Matthew 16:27, where Jesus says, "For the Son of Man is going to come in the glory of His Father with His angels and will then repay every man according to His deeds."

Make no mistake, government has its place—otherwise, God would never have instituted it to begin with (Romans 13). Nevertheless, that place is never to be in the place of God. God desires that people be treated equally as bearers of his image, but equality involves partiality, and partiality—of any kind—is sin.

A Basic Theology of Government

Given that government is God's idea (Romans 13:1), it is altogether right, proper, and even necessary that God's people hold to a proper theology of government and its divinely ordained role in the world. As John Calvin said, "The purpose of temporal government [as distinct from God's spiritual kingdom] is to fit us for human society for as long as we are a part of it, to teach us to behave equitably among men, to reconcile us with one another and to promote and preserve public peace and calm."[13]

It is in light of those words from Calvin that Christians would do well to keep the following realities in mind.

God Is Sovereign

To have a clear understanding regarding a theology of government, we must begin by understanding the sovereignty of God. In Genesis 1, God creates the world and everything in it. It is God who designs

---

13 Calvin, *Institutes of the Christian Religion*, 756.

"created order," and all things are subject to him. As an image-bearer, man is given dominion to rule God's creation in the manner God has determined. However, God is always completely sovereign.

Consider these texts for further study: Psalms 115:3; 103:19; 135:6; Proverbs 16:4; 19:21; Philippians 2:13; Colossians 1:16; Romans 11:36.

Man's Sinfulness Requires the Law

The result of the fall of mankind (Genesis 3) is devastating as sin begets lawlessness (1 John 3:4). As quickly as Genesis 4, we witness the first murder as mankind descends quickly into wickedness. Genesis 6:5 declares, "The LORD saw that the wickedness of mankind was great on the earth, and that every intent of the thoughts of their hearts was only evil continually."

It is important to note the condition of man's heart as sinfully wicked. Those seeking government as a complete solution for the problems of mankind must appeal to the objective standard of God rather than the subjective witness in the hearts of sinful human beings. Far too many people desire government solutions to problems that can only be remedied through transformed hearts. Chapter 6 of the 1689 London Baptist Confession captures the situation well: "By this sin our first parents fell from their original righteousness and communion with God. We fell in them, and through this, death came upon all. All became dead in sin and completely defiled in all the capabilities and parts of soul and body."[14]

As an act of grace, God gives the children of Israel the law. Moses delivers the commandments of God to the people. Moses then begins to establish a "government" as a judge of the people of Israel, in Exodus 18:15–26. There, we see that government serves as a warning to do what is right and as a deterrent against evil. Jethro, Moses's father-in-law, helps Moses establish the governance of the people. In verse 20, Jethro says, "You should explain God's laws and teachings

---

14 "The 1689 Baptist Confession of Faith in Modern English: Chapter 6: The Fall of Mankind, and Sin and Its Punishment," Founders Ministries, July 30, 2018, https://founders.org/library/1689-confession/chapter-6-the-fall-of-mankind-and-sin-and-its-punishment.

to the people. Warn them *not to break the laws*. Tell them the right way to live and what they should do" (ERV, emphasis added).

Government Is Established to Minimize Evil

Government as established by God is to promote righteousness and punish evil. Scripture is clear about this. Consider Romans 13:1–5:

> Let every person be subject to the governing authorities; for there is no authority except from God, and those authorities that exist have been instituted by God. Therefore whoever resists authority resists what God has appointed, and those who resist will incur judgment. For rulers are not a terror to good conduct, but to bad. Do you wish to have no fear of the authority? Then do what is good, and you will receive its approval; for it is God's servant for your good. But if you do what is wrong, you should be afraid, for the authority does not bear the sword in vain! It is the servant of God to execute wrath on the wrongdoer. Therefore one must be in subjection, not only because of wrath but also because of conscience. (NRSV)

Keep in mind that Paul isn't writing to the church in a democratic republic. This was God's instruction during the time of Roman rule, which could be oppressive and unfair. The act of submission to governmental authority is not the validation of government but rather an act of submission to God who is sovereign over all (Psalm 103:19).

Discussion Questions:

1. What is the difference between treating people equally and guaranteeing everyone equity?
2. Why is this distinction important to understanding the role of government?
3. What does Scripture have to say about the role of government? Does this include the redistribution of wealth?
4. What is every Christian's responsibility toward those who are poor?
5. In what fundamental ways does the gospel differ from the role of government?

Socialism

Socialism has become the new cultural buzzword. Everyone is talking about it. Everyone has an opinion. People assume they know what it is. But if you pay attention to the culture conversation, you'll discover there is a lot of confusion over the actual meaning of *socialism*. Unless you truly understand what socialism is by definition, anything you say about it is moot.

With that in mind, we open this chapter with a series of definitions, taking time to explain what socialism is before we examine how Scripture calls us to think about it.

What Is Socialism?

There are different types of socialism, so we will begin with a general definition. According to *Britannica*,

> socialism is a social and economic doctrine that calls for public rather than private ownership or control of property and natural resources. According to the socialist view, individuals do not live or work in isolation but live in cooperation with one another. Furthermore, everything that people produce is in some sense a social product, and everyone who contributes to the production of a good is entitled to a share equally in it. Society as a whole,

therefore, should own or at least control property for the benefit of all its members.¹

In other words, the socialist views individualism as wrong and regards collectivism as the goal. Capitalism looks at production and distribution of resources from an individual perspective. Socialism, however, looks at public and private ownership in the opposite way. It's a collective in which the rights of the government are first and the government redistributes wealth taken from individuals. Capitalism says, "You're an individual. You can control your own means of production, the distribution of those products, and the exchanges in which you'll engage. Those are all decided by you, the individual," while socialism says, "No, it's going to be decided by the collective, by the government entity, by the state."

Types of Socialism

In addition to presuming they understand the definition of socialism, many people assume there is only one type of socialism. This is a misunderstanding, as there are at least seven.

Democratic socialism advocates socialism as an economic principle in which the means of production should be in the hands of ordinary working people. It also considers democracy as a governing principle and attempts to bring about socialism through peaceful democratic means, such as elections, as opposed to violent insurrection. It is similar but not identical to *social democracy*, an ideology that is more centrist in nature and supports a broadly capitalist system, with some social reforms (such as the welfare state), intended to make society more equitable and humane. By contrast, democratic socialism embraces an ideology that is more left-wing and supportive of a fully socialist system, established either by gradually reforming capitalism from within or by some form of revolutionary transformation. Democratic socialists want to get rid of capitalism altogether through peaceful democratic means, such as voting.

---

1   Terence Ball and Richard Dagger, s.v., "socialism," *Encyclopedia Britannica*, March 1, 2021, https://www.britannica.com/topic/socialism.

This type of socialism is wildly popular in American society today and seems palatable to the masses because of the word *democratic*, which is merely one of the hooks, an example of terms employed by democratic socialists to appear innocuous. However, this type of socialism is no less destructive than the Marxist worldview from which it springs. Though it sounds nice and friendly with its "power to the people" message, this rhetoric is a subtle idea that traces right back to communism. In reality, the power is extracted from the people and given to the state. But this happens so deceptively that at the point at which people recognize they're in peril, it's already too late.

Revolutionary socialism advocates the need for fundamental social change through revolution or insurrection rather than gradual reform through the electoral process. We are seeing a current example of this in the Black Lives Matter activities—revolution, insurrection, agitation, confrontation. Revolutionary socialists want to go hard to transform society from capitalist to socialist. When revolutionary socialism calls for a fight to change society, literally, they want to fight.

Utopian socialism is a term used to define the first currents of modern socialist thought in the first quarter of the nineteenth century. Utopian socialism rejects all political and revolutionary action and seeks to attain its ends by peaceful means and small social experiments. Followers of this type of socialism want to build a socialist state piece by piece and block by block. They are not trying to change society on a rapid trajectory but are willing to wait it out.

Libertarian socialism seeks to create a society without political, economic, or social hierarchies, one in which every person would have free and equal access to tools of information and production. This would be achieved through the abolition of authoritarian institutions and private property so that direct control of the means of production and resources will be gained by the working class and society as a whole. Again, the theme of promoting collectivism over individualism is clearly evident.

Market socialism is a term used to define an economic system in which there is a market economy directed and guided by socialist planners. Here prices would be set through trial and error, with adjustments made as shortages and surpluses occur, rather than relying on a free-price or "free market" mechanism. This is different from a *socialist market economy* (as practiced in the People's Republic of China) in which major industries are owned by the state but compete with each other within a pricing system set by the market. Market socialism takes advantage of the fact that capitalism has built-in inequities. These inequities exist because capitalists are sinners. When inequities appear in a capitalist system, the market socialists show up on the scene, and what they have to say may sound really good. But their finger pointing is merely a smoke screen designed to distract from the reality of socialism, which is absolutely flawed in its nature.

Eco-socialism (also known as green socialism or socialist ecology) is an ideology merging aspects of Marxism, socialism, green politics, and aspects of the climate change and anti-globalization movements. Eco-socialists advocate the nonviolent dismantling of capitalism and the state, focusing on collective ownership of the means of production to mitigate the social exclusion, poverty, and environmental degradation brought about, as they see it, by the capitalist system, globalization, and imperialism. This is the type of socialism being advocated and propagated by New York congresswoman Alexandria Ocasio-Cortez in the Green New Deal, which is the epitome of eco-socialism.[2]

Christian Socialism

The final type of socialism is where we will focus most of our attention because this is the socialism that is being most embraced by the evangelical church today. *Christian socialism* refers to those on the Christian sociopolitical left whose worldview is a hybrid of both biblical Christianity and socialism and who see these two things as being interconnected within the teachings of Jesus Christ. Christian socialists draw parallels between what some have characterized as the egalitarian and anti-establishment message of Jesus, and the messages of modern socialism. It is somewhat of a hybrid worldview, a comingling of socialism with a confused understanding of the gospel message.

---

2 See "Green New Deal," Green Party US, https://www.gp.org/green_new_deal.

This, of all the various aspects of socialism, is the most dangerous as it attempts to add to the pure gospel. The gospel is the only thing in this world that changes hearts and minds and rights all that is wrong with a fallen humanity. When we begin mixing the gospel with something as pernicious and antithetical to biblical Christianity as socialism, we incur the curse of Paul to the Galatian church: "But even if we, or an angel from heaven, should preach to you a gospel contrary to what we have preached to you, he is to be accursed!" (Galatians 1:8). A hybrid of socialism and Christianity deserves such a response. Unfortunately, it is this very hybrid that many liberal evangelical Christians are advocating under the banner of the "social gospel." The social gospel is nothing more than Christian socialism under a different name.

The origins of the social gospel date back to the early nineteenth century and Christian progressives such as Washington Gladden, William Dwight Porter Bliss, and Walter Rauschenbusch. The social gospel movement was a response to the rapid urbanization, industrialization, and mass immigration of the late 1800s when Protestant clergymen became interested in securing social justice for the poor. It was partly as an attempt to expand the appeal of the Protestant church in urban cities where the Roman Catholic Church was especially popular among large immigrant populations.

Traditionally, the social gospel has focused on issues as varied as poverty, unemployment, civil rights, pollution, drug addiction, political corruption, and gun control. It rejects the individualistic social ethic, adhering instead to a distinctively collectivist rationale. This is a direct result of the theological liberalism that emerged from attempts to reconcile the Christian faith with evolutionary thought, historical-critical analysis of the Bible, philosophical idealism, and the study of other world religions. It is much more worldly than gospel.

At the core of the social gospel is the idea that Christians must work in this world to establish the kingdom of God with social justice for all—which, today, includes reparations for slavery as well as ecclesiastical egalitarianism. The influence of theological liberalism is obvious.

Against Christian Socialism

One of the more vociferous opponents of Christian socialism was a man by the name of Frederick Nymeyer. In the 1950s and 1960s, Nymeyer was the publisher and principal author of a publication called *Progressive Calvinism*. In 1971, in a paper titled "Social Action, Hundred Nineteen," Nymeyer wrote,

> The Social gospel may be the most crucial of all problems besetting Christian churches at this time, for when a Christian's ethical certitudes are revealed to be defective, as it always turns out to be in the Social gospel, then he ends up abandoning confidence in valid, biblical faith. In practice what happens is that when Social gospel action fails to produce valid results, the person promoting such programs does not abandon the Social gospel and return to the true gospel, but plunges deeper into further Social gospel actions with progressively more frustrating results. No denomination appears to have prospered greatly, in ideas or in peace, under the Social gospel. There is reason to believe that the consequences of the irrationalism of the Social gospel may turn out to be as unfavorable in the Christian Reformed Church as they have been elsewhere.[3]

Following the same train of thought as Nymeyer, D. Martyn Lloyd-Jones, in his book *Preaching & Preachers*, wrote,

> I have no hesitation in asserting that what was largely responsible for emptying the churches in Great Britain was that "social gospel" preaching and the institutional church. It was more responsible for doing so than anything else. The people rightly argued in this way, that if the business of the Church was really just to preach a form of political and social reform and pacifism then the Church was not really necessary, for all this could have been done through political agencies. So they left the churches and went and did it, or tried to do it, through their political parties. That was perfectly logical, but its effect upon the churches was most harmful. When you depart from the primary task of the Church and do something else, though your motive may be pure and excellent, that is the result. I am not disputing or criticizing the

---

[3] Quoted in Bill Moyers, "The Social Gospel Tradition," *Bill Moyers Journal*, July 3, 2009, https://www.pbs.org/moyers/journal/07032009/profile2.html.

motives, I am simply showing that actually this theory in practice has the reverse effect from that which it sets out to achieve. I argue that in many ways it is the departure of the Church from preaching that is responsible in a large measure for the state of modern society. The church has been trying to preach morality and ethics without the gospel as a basis; it has been preaching morality without godliness; and it simply does not work. It never has done, and it never will. And the result is that the Church, having abandoned *her real task*, has left humanity more or less to its own devices.[4]

Consider that Nymeyer and Lloyd-Jones said these things half a century ago. Scripture is clear; "there is nothing new under the sun" (Ecclesiastes 1:9). According to Lloyd-Jones, the social gospel is "largely responsible for emptying the churches in Great Britain." What we are seeing in our time is the same. And when adherents of Christian socialism find it's not working, rather than correct their thinking, they double and triple down.

Millennial Attraction

Despite the differences of the various types of socialism we've covered, when all is said and done, they all have one fundamental objective in common: the confiscation and redistribution of individual wealth and the control and/or elimination of private property. That is the endgame of all socialistic ideologies, regardless of the differences in their approach. A case in point is some information available on the website SocialistWorker.org: "War, poverty, exploitation, oppression and worldwide environmental destruction are products of the capitalist system, a system in which a minority ruling class profits from the labor of the majority. The alternative is socialism, a society based on workers collectively owning and controlling the wealth their labor creates. We stand in the Marxist tradition, founded by Karl Marx and Frederick Engels, and continued by V.I. Lenin, Rosa Luxemburg and Leon Trotsky."[5]

---

[4] D. Martyn Lloyd-Jones, *Preaching & Preachers: The Classic Text with Essays from Mark Dever, Kevin DeYoung, Timothy Keller, John Piper, and Others* (Grand Rapids: Zondervan, 2011), 44–45.

[5] "Where We Stand," SocialistWorker.org, accessed June 15, 2021, https://socialistworker.org/where-we-stand.

This idea of wealth redistribution seems especially popular today among the young. An article that appeared on the website *The Federalist* in 2015 included survey data that showed that 53 percent of eighteen- to twenty-nine-year-olds had a favorable view of socialism compared to only 25 percent of Americans over age fifty-five.[6] A primary reason so many millennials are attracted to socialism is because they don't actually understand what socialism is.

Additional sources confirm this. When confronted with the actual definition of socialism—government ownership of the means of production, or government running businesses—only 32 percent of millennials favor "an economy managed by the government" while, similar to older generations, 64 percent prefer a free-market economy.[7] And as millennials age and begin to earn more, "their socialistic ideals seem to slip away."[8] Why is that? Because of an innate awareness that the wages for which one labors honestly and legally belong to the laborer and not the state. Millennials know instinctively that when you put forth your own volitional labor and are compensated for it, your wages belong to you. They don't belong to the government. This is an inherent principle that is understood naturally; you don't need to go to school to learn it.

When millennials are brought face-to-face with what socialism is *as an ideology*, their support for the concept of centralized state ownership of their labor, productivity, and property drops by more than 20 percent. It is vital to understand the concepts of any doctrine to which you hold, which is why we took the time at the beginning of this chapter to define what socialism actually is and to distinguish between some of the various types of socialism that exist today.

---

6 Emily Ekins and Joy Pullmann, "Why So Many Millennials Are Socialists," *The Federalist*, February 25, 2016, https://thefederalist.com/2016/02/15/why-so-many-millennials-are-socialists; Emily Ekins, "Poll: Americans Like Free Markets More than Capitalism and Socialism More Than a Govt Managed Economy," Reason, February 12, 2015), https://reason.com/2015/02/12/poll-americans-like-free-markets-more-th.
7 Emily Ekins, "Millennials Don't Know What 'Socialism' Means," Reason, July 16, 2014, https://reason.com/2014/07/16/millennials-dont-know-what-socialism-mea.
8 Emily Ekins, "Opinion: Millennials like socialism—until they get jobs," *The Washington Post*, March 24, 2016, https://www.washingtonpost.com/news/in-theory/wp/2016/03/24/millennials-like-socialism-until-they-get-jobs.

Socialism sounds great when you are thinking about getting a share of other people's property for free. Today, more and more eighteen- to twenty-nine-year-olds haven't lived on their own for very long, having stayed at home longer than previous generations, with their health insurance and other costs of living maintained by their parents. Under those conditions, it is easy to subscribe to an ideology that promises more free stuff for a longer amount of time. When you are the one responsible for creating the earnings that support someone else, however, socialism doesn't sound so favorable. When you become a wage earner, you recognize that whatever you earn, you'd like to keep. Unsurprisingly, socialistic ideas begin to wane when we recognize the actual realities socialism brings.

The Doctrine of Socialism

Britannica rightly defines *socialism* as a "doctrine that calls for public rather than private ownership or control of property and natural resources."[9] Winston Churchill used the word *philosophy* instead when he said, "Socialism is a philosophy of failure, the creed of ignorance, and the gospel of envy."[10] And what exactly is meant by *doctrine* or *philosophy*? It is simply a body or collection of teachings related to a particular subject.

Socialism is a doctrine, a creed. It is a philosophy, an ideology, a worldview. It is a philosophical paradigm through which increasing numbers of people, including many who profess to be Christians, see the world. There are those in America and the church today who hold to a socialist worldview and are employing their time, energy, and money to ensure that worldview succeeds where other attempts have failed.

Those in the church must take this seriously. Consider how those outside the church have evaluated the socialist ideology. Twentieth-century Marxist economist Ernest Mandel said, "Socialist democracy is not a luxury but an absolute, essential necessity for overthrowing

---

9 Ball and Dagger, "socialism."
10 "Perth, Scotland, 28 May 1948," in Churchill, *Europe Unite: Speeches 1947 & 1948* (London: Cassell, 1950), 347.

capitalism and building socialism."[11] Aldous Huxley, an English writer and philosopher, weighed in on the idea of communal ownership: "It is only when we have renounced our preoccupation with 'I,' 'me,' 'mine,' that we can truly possess the world in which we live. Everything is ours, provided that we regard nothing as our property. And not only is everything ours; it is also everybody else's."[12] Finally, Russian-American writer and philosopher Ayn Rand coolly compared socialism and communism: "There is no difference between communism and socialism, except in the means of achieving the same ultimate end: communism proposes to enslave men by force, socialism—by vote. It is merely the difference between murder and suicide."[13]

The doctrinal nature of socialism is further evidenced by the list of causes supported by the International Socialists Organization (ISO). According to their website, ISO champions the following: women's liberation, fighting racism, LGBTQ liberation, building a socialist alternative, anti-imperialism and international solidarity, the labor movement, climate and environmental justice, education justice, Palestinian rights, disability rights, indigenous rights, and independent political action.[14]

This list is enlightening on a number of levels, most significantly as one realizes that the whole point of isolating individuals into separate collectives is to overthrow the capitalist system. This isolation is not for the purpose of individual rights or to help individuals within these groups but to promote a collective identity. For example, rather than being Virgil and Darrell, individuals, under the socialist worldview driving the ISO, we would become black men marginalized by a culture that now needs to be overthrown. The point of this redefined identity is that individuals would sign on to the socialist collective

---

11 Ernest Mandel, "Vanguard Parties," *Mid-American Review of Sociology* VIII, no. 2 (1983), 3–21, https://www.ernestmandel.org/en/works/txt/1983/vanguard_parties.htm.
12 Aldous Huxley, *The Perennial Philosophy* (London: Chatto & Windus, 1947), 125.
13 Ayn Rand, "Foreign Policy Drains U.S. of Main Weapon," *The Los Angeles Times*, September 1962, G2.
14 "Topics," SocialistWorker.org, accessed June 14, 2021, https://socialistworker.org/topic.

agenda. And the best way to get you to accept this ideology is to dupe you into believing something about yourself that is not true.

While we wholeheartedly disavow the doctrine of socialism with every fiber of our beings, the ISO does get one thing correct: capitalism cannot meet human needs. We completely agree. But neither can socialism, Marxism, Confucianism, Maoism, Taoism, Hinduism, Buddhism, fascism, communism—or any other worldly -*ism*, for that matter. This reality prompts an essential question: If none of these things meets human needs—and they don't—then what is it that humanity *truly* needs, and is there anything today that *can* meet those needs? The answer, of course, is found in the truth of the gospel, which stands in stark contrast to the doctrine of socialism.

Socialism Is Unbiblical

A primary reason many professing Christians are buying into the doctrine of socialism and the social gospel is they mistakenly believe that societal egalitarianism is the primary goal of the gospel. They believe that the church should be actively endeavoring to establish the kingdom of God on earth, not only by meeting the spiritual needs of people but also by meeting all felt needs and material wants. Meeting these needs and wants should be done by almost any means necessary, including the confiscation and redistribution of individual wealth and private property by the government. Yet this is wholly antithetical to what the gospel teaches:

> For you yourselves know how you ought to follow our example, because we did not act in an undisciplined way among you, nor did we eat anyone's bread without paying for it, but with labor and hardship we kept working night and day so that we would not be a burden to any of you; not because we do not have the right to this, but in order to offer ourselves as a role model for you, so that you would follow our example. For even when we were with you, we used to give you this order: if anyone is not willing to work, then he is not to eat, either. For we hear that some among you are leading an undisciplined life, doing no work at all, but acting like busybodies. Now we command and exhort such persons in the Lord Jesus Christ to work in quiet fashion and eat their own bread. (2 Thessalonians 3:7–12)

Much in this text is clearly adverse to socialism, so let's exposit it at a high level:

- The words "anyone's bread" uses the possessive pronoun ("anyone's"), which implies the idea of private ownership of property ("bread").
- The phrase "without paying for it" conveys the same idea as the eighth commandment in Exodus 20:15, "You shall not steal," as well as the imperative from the apostle Paul in Ephesians 4:28, "The one who steals must no longer steal; but rather he must labor, producing with his own hands what is good, so that he will have something to share with one who has need."
- The phrases "with labor and hardship" and "working day and night" carry with them the idea that Christians are to be determined and intentional in putting forth every possible effort to legitimately provide for themselves so as to not place a financial burden on anyone else, even if it means personal hardship in doing so.
- The phrase "eat their own bread" conveys the idea that one must work to acquire their own property, whether it be food or otherwise, and need is no excuse for taking from someone else that which does not rightfully belong to you.

Scripture clearly teaches that believers in Christ should be willing to work so they can "eat their own bread," not someone else's. The word "willing" in the text above is the Greek verb *thelō*, which translated means "to be resolved or determined to do a thing." Notice that twice in 2 Thessalonians 3:7–12 the apostle Paul equates an unwillingness to work with leading an "undisciplined life." The word "undisciplined" (*atakteō*) is a military term that describes soldiers who are deliberately neglectful in carrying out their assigned duties, obligations, and responsibilities.

The principle here is pretty clear. Paul exhorts those undisciplined people to work in quiet fashion and eat their own bread, not someone else's.

Private Ownership Is Biblical

This text and so many others presuppose private ownership and assume that we are to give under our own volition. Scripture clearly states that God loves a cheerful giver (2 Corinthians 9:7), indicating that we are individuals who have rights to our own wealth and are under no compulsion to give. For Christian social justicians to say that it is a gospel imperative that we do X, Y, or Z for those who don't have is antithetical to these Scripture suppositions about ownership and giving.

Even John Calvin had to deal with this issue in his day, writing in *Institutes of the Christian Religion*, "[Government] is not merely concerned with what people eat and drink and with how life is sustained, although it includes all those things by allowing men to live together. It involves more than that: it aims to see . . . that each person *keeps what is his* and that men live together without injury or dishonesty; in short, that among Christians there should be an open expression of religion, and that in society humanity should prevail."[15] Calvin is arguing here for the biblical concept of property. We know from Romans 13 that the principle of government was instituted by God and that every government that exists on this planet is providentially established by him. Calvin says that one of the responsibilities of divinely established government is to ensure that each person keeps what is his. Nowhere in Scripture is government tasked with the responsibility of meeting the practical needs of people. For those who are able to work, the responsibility falls to them *individually* to make a living for themselves and provide their own well-being ("bread"), even if it means suffering hardship in doing so. Those who are able but are unwilling to work will suffer the consequences of their sinful laziness. Proverbs 19:15 says, "Laziness casts one into a deep sleep, and a lazy person will suffer hunger." Likewise, Proverbs 14:23 says, "In all labor there is profit, but mere talk leads only to poverty."

---

15 John Calvin, *Institutes of the Christian Religion*, trans. Robert White (Edinburgh: Banner of Truth, 2014), 4.20.2 (emphasis added).

Ecclesiastical Responsibility

As we touched on in chapter 1, the responsibility for those who are unable to work falls to the church, never to the government. A case in point is Paul's instruction in 1 Timothy 5:3, "Honor widows who are widows indeed," and in verse 5 of that same chapter, "Now she who is a widow indeed and who has been left alone, has fixed her hope on God and continues in entreaties and prayers night and day." Additionally, in verse 16 of 1 Timothy 5 Paul writes, "If any woman who is a believer has dependent widows, she must assist them and the church must not be burdened, so that it may assist those who are widows indeed."

Three times in 1 Timothy 5 Paul uses the word "indeed" (*ontōs*) concerning widows, which speaks of women who are *actually* widows. What Paul is saying is that to the extent the church is responsible for caring for widows and others who would petition the church for assistance, those needs must be legitimate and qualifiable. In other words, one cannot simply claim to be in need and expect the church to come to the rescue. In fact, Paul makes it clear, as we just read in 1 Timothy 5:16, that some needs not even the church is responsible for, or else it would be hindered from meeting more pressing needs of women who are "widows indeed." Paul says, "If any woman who is a believer has dependent widows, she must assist them and the church must not be burdened."

This is an area of *ecclesiology*, what the church is to do (and not do), and how individuals who represent the church are to respond to those who have needs. It requires the believer in Christ to really know their Bible, understand it, and be ready to act and respond to those they see who have legitimate needs, while understanding that the local church is not called to address every need or want around it.

Socialism's Fundamental Flaw

The gospel is inherently volitional—compulsive only by virtue of our love for Christ rather than coercive. In contrast, socialism is inherently coercive. Evangelical social justicians try to lay a guilt trip on individuals, burdening them with pseudo-guilt, virtual guilt, that isn't theirs. There is no difference between that and the guilt-tripping socialism of the world.

The gospel does what socialism can't. A leading Chinese scholar quoted in David Aikman's book *Jesus in Beijing: How Christianity Is Changing the Global Balance of Power* remarked,

> One of the things we were asked to look into was what accounted for the success, in fact, the pre-eminence of the West all over the world. We studied everything we could from the historical, political, economic, and cultural perspective. At first, we thought it was because you had more powerful guns than we had. Then we thought it was because you had the best political system. Next we focused on your economic system. But in twenty years, we have realized that the heart of your culture is your religion: Christianity. That is why the West is so powerful. The Christian moral foundation of social and cultural life was what made possible the emergence of capitalism and then the successful transition to democratic politics. We don't have any doubt about this.[16]

A fundamental fallacy of socialism is that it promises that which it cannot possibly deliver—an egalitarian society devoid of consequences for sin. If you don't want to work, no problem; socialism forces others to work *for you* so you can reap the benefits of their efforts. But it will also force you to work for others so they can reap the benefits of your efforts. Consider these words from Proverbs 5:21–23: "For the ways of a man are before the eyes of the Lord, and He watches all his paths. His own iniquities will capture the wicked, and he will be held with the cords of his sin. He will die for lack of instruction, and in the greatness of his folly he will go astray."

Socialists would have you believe that socialism is *cool*, that it is the best way to live in the world today. This is the message that more than half of millennials have bought into, until, that is, they are confronted with the real definition of socialism or until they are forced to cough up money from their own pockets to pay for the wants and needs of

---

16 David Aikman, *Jesus in Beijing: How Christianity Is Changing the Global Balance of Power* (Washington, DC: Salem Books, 2012), 5.

others. It's then they discover that Nobel prize-winning economist F. A. Hayek was right when he said, "Socialism means slavery."[17]

In contrast, the Bible places value on human liberty, as Wayne Grudem explains:

> The Bible's teaching on the role of government gives support to the idea of a free market rather than socialism or communism. This is because nothing in the Bible's teachings on the role of government would give the government warrant to take over ownership or control of private businesses (or property). The government is to punish evil and reward those who do good and enforce order in our society. It is not to own people's private property or businesses. The Bible's emphasis on the value of human liberty also argues for a free market system rather than a socialist or communist system. A free market allows individuals to choose where they work, what they buy, how they run a business, and how they spend *their* money. But a government-controlled economy makes these decisions *for* people rather than allowing people the freedom to make decisions for themselves.[18]

In the words of William Ellery Channing, "The office of government does not exist to confer happiness but to give men opportunity to work out happiness for themselves."[19]

The Lie of Socialism

Socialism is a lie. It is a mirage. It is an ideology that collapses on itself. It is built on the contradiction that under the guise of morality and the pursuit of a more equitable society, it is permissible to act immorally and to steal from one group of people to enrich another. But theft is not the means by which God would have us pursue a more just and equitable society.

---

17 Thomas W. Hazlett, "F. A. Hayek: Classical Liberal," FEE, September 1, 1979, https://fee.org/articles/f-a-hayek-classical-liberal.
18 Wayne Grudem, *Politics According to the Bible: A Comprehensive Resource for Understanding Modern Political Issues in Light of Scripture* (Grand Rapids: Zondervan, 2010), 275–276 (emphasis added).
19 Wiliam Ellery Channing, "Review of The Life of Napoleon Bonaparte (1827) by Sir Walter Scott," *The Christian Examiner* (September–October 1827).

God's design for those who desire a just and equal society is two-pronged. First, come to faith in Jesus Christ and confess him as Savior and Lord (Romans 10:9–10). Second, commit to obey Jesus's word, which says, "You shall not steal" what rightfully belongs to someone else (Exodus 20:15) or covet what someone else has (Exodus 20:17).

Paul's letter to the church at Galatia explains how the people of God, who have put their faith in Christ and are committed to obeying his word, impact their society: "Let us not lose heart in doing good, for in due time we will reap if we do not grow weary. So then, while we have opportunity, let us do good to all people, and especially to those who are of the household of the faith" (Galatians 6:9–10). In other words, "the love of Christ controls us" (2 Corinthians 5:14), not the government. The gospel calls us to reject the false doctrine of socialism and meet people's needs out of our love for Christ.

Discussion Questions

1. Based on this chapter, what is the definition of "socialism"?
2. What are the five types of socialism defined in the chapter?
3. What are the arguments in favor of Christian socialism? What are the arguments against Christian socialism?
4. According to the reading, why are millennials attracted to Christian socialism?
5. What is socialism's fundamental flaw and the lie adopted by culture?

Capitalism

In Genesis 1:27–28, God completes the crown of his creation, mankind, and gives them an important directive: "God created man in His own image, in the image of God He created him; male and female He created them. God blessed them; and God said to them, 'Be fruitful and multiply and fill the earth and subdue it; and rule over the fish of the sea and over the birds of the sky and over every living thing that moves on the earth.'"

Now, some readers may be thinking, "Are Virgil and Darrell really trying to say that God is a capitalist, and are they really going to use Genesis 1:27 and following to make that case?" Well, our answer to that is no, we don't believe that God is a capitalist. But we do intend to make the argument that the fundamental tenets of capitalism begin with a proper biblical worldview, understanding that it pertains to the sovereignty of God, not government, and the stewardship of man, not members of Congress.

What Is Capitalism?

We always want to begin any discussion by defining our terms, so we must start by answering the question, "What is capitalism?"

According to economist, professor, and author Dr. Fred Foldvary, "'capitalism' means the sector of an economy in which markets [not government] determine prices and quantities. In a 'capitalist' system both the market for goods and the market for inputs are based on voluntary action within the constraints of some governmental interventions, namely taxes, subsidies, restrictions, and mandates."[1] In other words, in a capitalist system, both items purchased ("the market for goods") and needs to be fulfilled ("the market for inputs") are based on voluntary actions. We have a need; you have a good. You will produce goods based on what we need, and we will seek the fulfillment of our needs through the goods you provide. These are voluntary actions within the constraints of the government interventions listed above.

Webster's further defines *capitalism* as "an economic system characterized by private or corporate ownership of capital goods, by investments that are determined by private decisions, and by prices, production, and the distribution of goods that are determined mainly by competition in a free market."[2] Again, these are voluntary actions taken on by the individual within the marketplace. These are private decisions and transactions, the price of which is determined by the individuals in the system. There must be a mutually beneficial exchange.

It is also helpful to have a clear understanding of *capital* and *capitalist*. Capital is basically defined as wealth—that is, money and goods—that's used to produce more wealth. On the term *capitalist*, Foldvary provides some interesting comments, saying, "The term 'capitalism' was first used in 1854 by William Thackeray in his novel *The Newcomes*. The term 'capitalist' was used previously to refer to an owner of capital goods. The term was popularized by the German sociologist Max Weber as well as by other socialists who use the term to condemn private enterprise as a system that exploits labor. In response, advocates of free markets use the term to mean private enterprise and to praise the concept of a free-market economy."[3]

---

1 Fred Foldvary PhD, "Capitalism Defined and Explained," Progress, July 19, 2015, https://www.progress.org/articles/capitalism-defined-and-explained.
2 *Merriam-Webster*, s.v. "capitalism," accessed June 14, 2021, https://www.merriam-webster.com/dictionary/capitalism.
3 Foldvary, "Capitalism."

In the media today we often hear advocates of alternative economic systems do exactly what Thackeray and others did with regard to free markets in the 1850s. They label *capitalism* as negative and attach to it other pejorative terms in an effort to expose its excesses, all the while arguing that the excesses are representative of the whole.

In these instances, you hear terms like *crony capitalism*. Socialists, anarchists, communists, and all those opposed to a capitalist system will employ this term as a blanket definition. This is merely using the excesses of the system to characterize the whole of capitalism. In true crony capitalism, the government shows preferential treatment through intervention regarding fixed regulation, special taxation, and other forms of corporate privilege. The truth is that crony capitalism can only take place where the government has an overreaching ability to intervene and reduce the risk inherent in a free market. It's not a form of capitalism—it's fundamentally anti-capitalist.

Consider this hypothetical: a capitalist decides he wants to advance in business. But rather than engage in the free market system, he invests in someone he knows campaigning for a particular position in political office. Once that politician is in office, he, in turn, does a favor for the capitalist who helped him get to his position. Perhaps the politician creates laws that unfairly advantage a particular business or company. That's crony capitalism. Perhaps he uses government funds to purchase the products made by the capitalist who helped put him in office. That's also crony capitalism. But crony capitalism only happens due to the overreach of government in the first place, mitigating the risk of a free market economy.

Capitalism is best discussed in terms of free market economies, but at best, the current American system is more of a mixed economy. Much of the economy is free and open without the government setting prices and private individuals still owning and producing as they see fit. This free market, however, stands alongside government intervention that, depending on the party in power, seems to be ever increasing by the day.

Having defined our terms, let's go back to our initial premise: the fundamental tenets of capitalism begin with a proper biblical worldview, understanding that it pertains to the sovereignty of God, not government, and the stewardship of man, not members of Congress.

A Biblical Worldview: The Sovereignty of God

To begin, we return to Genesis 1:27–28: "God created man in His own image, in the image of God He created him; male and female He created them. God blessed them; and God said to them, 'Be fruitful and multiply and fill the earth and subdue it; and rule over the fish of the sea and over the birds of the sky and over every living thing that moves on the earth.'"

Compare this passage with Proverbs 22:2, which says, "The rich and the poor have a common bond, the LORD is the Maker of them all." What both these texts point to is the fact that God is sovereign over all he has made, including mankind. This is a core element of a biblical worldview.

Why start a discussion of capitalism there? Because those who founded our country—as flawed as some would argue they were—got some things right. One of those things was that they held to a biblical worldview in the founding of a nation. The founders, from the Puritans to the pilgrims to the signers of the Declaration of Independence, understood and held to a biblical understanding of God's sovereignty. They embraced the fundamental notion that God controlled everything and they were but stewards of that creation. It was clear to those men that apart from God and our continued focus on him, we would be lost as a nation.

This idea of God's sovereignty in all things can be traced back to the very beginning of the founding of our nation. The first of the founding documents was written in 1620 by the 102 passengers of the *Mayflower*. What would come to be known as the Mayflower Compact spelled out the reason that this group and many others after them would leave the Old World and embark upon the New. While we call them pilgrims, the nearly 40 passengers who were Protestant separatists called themselves "Saints" and hoped to establish a new life and a new church away from the persecution of their homeland.

The Mayflower Compact reads "In the name of God, Amen. We, whose names are underwritten . . . have undertaken for the Glory of God, and the Advancement of the Christian Faith, and the Honour of our King and Country, a Voyage to plant the first Colony in the northern Parts of Virginia; Do by these Presents, solemnly and mutually, in the Presence of God and one another, covenant and combine ourselves together into a civil Body Politick, for our better Ordering and Preservation."

Look at the purpose these pilgrims gave for coming to this new place. They had undertaken the voyage for the glory of God and the advancement of the gospel. They also did this in honor of the king and country from which they had come to plant a specific colony. They covenanted in the presence of God and one another to form their government with the purpose of order and preservation.

Why cite these examples? We want it to be clear that from the first governmental document originating in the New World, the signers put forward their goal to glorify God and further the Christian faith. They rooted the government of their new colony in the knowledge of God's sovereign rule over them.

It is fascinating to note that not only the pilgrims held to a biblical view that all they did was for the glory of God. Those who would be signers of the Declaration of Independence also held a similar worldview about God's sovereignty and their role in the order of that sovereignty. Take, for example, John Adams, who would later become the second president of the United States. In a letter to a family member written on June 21, 1776, Adams wrote, "Statesmen my dear Sir, may plan and speculate for Liberty, but it is Religion and Morality alone, which can establish the Principles upon which Freedom can securely stand."[4] In considering what liberty is truly all about, Adams settled on the reality that only a biblical worldview ("Religion and Morality alone") could support the freedom and independence on which the country was embarking.

---

4 John Adams, "John Adams to Zabdiel Adams, 21 June 1776," *Founders Online*, National Archives, https://founders.archives.gov/documents/Adams/04-02-02-0011.

Adams, who had entered Harvard College in 1751 at the age of sixteen, had been inculcated with a biblical worldview. The vast majority of education at this time was filled with the tenets of the Christian faith. Throughout the colonial period, from early education and the *New England Primer* (which taught children to read and write) to the leading college of the day, Harvard, the biblical worldview was clearly evident. In fact, the Harvard Rules and Precepts of 1646 read "Let every student be plainly instructed, and earnestly pressed to consider well the main end of his life and studies is to know God and Jesus Christ which is eternal life [John 17:3], and therefore lay Christ in the bottom as the only foundation of all sound knowledge and learning."[5] Harvard, the oldest institution of higher learning in America, was founded by Puritans who anticipated the need for training clergy in the New World and believed a biblical worldview was imperative.

We could further prove the point by quoting other founders, such as Benjamin Rush, who said, "Christianity is the only true and perfect religion, and that in proportion as mankind adopts its principles, and obey its precepts, they will be wise, and happy."[6] Or Charles Carroll, another signer of the Declaration of Independence, who observed, "Without morals, a republic cannot subsist any length of time; they therefore who are decrying the Christian religion . . . are undermining the solid foundation of morals, the best security for the duration of free governments."[7]

Here is the point we're making: those who founded our country held to a biblical worldview that set the stage for the ideas surrounding free markets, limited government, and the importance of God as the Sovereign to whom we all will give an account.

---

5 David Roth, "Harvard University Rules & Precepts," Christian Heritage Academy, July 20, 2016, https://christianheritage.org/harvard-university-rules-precepts.
6 Benjamin Rush, *Essays, Literary, Moral and Philosophical*, 2nd ed. (Philadelphia: Thomas and William Bradford, 1806), 93.
7 Charles Carroll, "Letter to James McHenry, 4 November 1800," *The Life and Correspondence of James McHenry* (Burrows Brothers Company, 1907), 475.

A Biblical Worldview: The Stewardship of Man

Now we turn to the latter half of our premise, which is that a biblical worldview teaches the stewardship of man (individual), not members of Congress (collective).

Let us begin by reading Exodus 20:9–10: "Six days you shall labor and do all your work, but the seventh day is a sabbath of the LORD your God; in it you shall not do any work, you or your son or your daughter, your male or your female servant or your cattle or your sojourner who stays with you." We could also have gone back to Genesis 2:15, where God puts the man in the garden of Eden and commands him to work it and keep it.

The point here is that it is God who ordains work, not greedy capitalists. God did not design work *after* the fall but *before* it; work is a blessing. After the fall in Genesis 3, work is still in view; however, we are told that, because of the curse, it will become more difficult.

All our work is done under the authority and view of God. Unfortunately, we live in a culture that seems to abhor work and is continuing to grow in disdain for it. In contrast, consider what the Bible says, particularly in the book of Proverbs:

- "Do you see a man skilled in his work? He will stand before kings; he will not stand before obscure men" (Proverbs 22:29).
- "In all labor there is profit, but mere talk leads only to poverty. The crown of the wise is their riches, but the folly of fools is foolishness" (Proverbs 14:23–24).

What we see in these proverbs is that work is a blessing, placing the skillful man before kings.

- "He who tills his land will have plenty of food, but he who follows empty pursuits will have poverty in plenty" (Proverbs 28:19).

Within this one verse of Scripture, we have land ownership and the blessing of work. We also have the acknowledgment that some pursuits are worthless and those worthless pursuits deserve the poverty that follows. Allow us to cite a few examples of this from our nation's history.

First, we must say that the Founding Fathers of our country did not practice free market capitalism but rather perfected it from a mercantile exchange that included government intervention and heavy taxation. Some of you may recall from your history books the infamous Boston Tea Party that occurred on December 16, 1773, at Griffin's Wharf in Boston, Massachusetts. The American colonists, led by a group known as the Sons of Liberty, dumped 342 chests of British tea into the harbor (some estimate the adjusted value at more than $1 million today). Why were the colonists so upset? Britain had a great deal of debt from recent wars. In an effort to decrease the debt, heavy taxes were levied against colonists in America, affecting everything from printed paper to playing cards. The Townshend Acts of 1767 taxed essentials such as paint, paper, glass, lead, and tea, which was particularly infuriating to the colonists. These taxes came without any representation of the American colonists in the British Parliament. The colonists were fed up with taxation without representation, which was seen as government overreach. Events escalated to the Boston Tea Party and, eventually, the American Revolutionary War. The mercantile system, with its heavy taxation and government involvement, provided a critical element of the environment for the Tea Party and all that followed.

In addition to the mercantile system, some forms of communal living in early American history resulted in starvation and devastation. It was the socialism of its day. People would gather in communes, and everyone would work, dividing up the resources from their labor. The problem was that some would work hard and others would not. But regardless of how hard one worked and how little another worked, they all got an even share. It was a socialism experiment that had been tried before and failed. One of the original signatories of the Mayflower Compact, William Bradford, observed this tragic failure. Later, as governor of Plymouth Colony, Bradford was asked about the tragic failure of communal living. He replied, "By adopting the communal system we thought we were wiser than God."[8] Why would

---

8 William Bradford, *Of Plymouth Plantation* (New York: Capricorn, 1962), 120–121.

he say that? Because he understood the biblical worldview and had deviated from it through the practice of socialism by communal living.

Questions about Capitalism

At this point we want to examine what some argue are the abuses of free market capitalism. Detractors of capitalism posit that the capitalistic system is full of evil, selfish rich people who abuse others and steal from the have-nots in order to fulfill their materialistic lusts. Granted, capitalism, like any system, is filled with sinful people who desire all kinds of immoral things. But to assume that another system, such as socialism, is inherently moral and devoid of the effect of sinful humans is foolish and dangerously destructive.

The charge by many is that capitalism is a system where the greedy take advantage of the weak for the benefit of the few. On its face, this is false. Capitalism involves the free exchange of goods and services. No one is forced to purchase anything. It's socialism that requires the exchange of goods and services at a price determined by the government at the point of a gun.

Recall the previous chapter where we cited an article from *The Federalist* on socialism, which included survey data that showed that 53 percent of eighteen- to twenty-nine-year-olds had a favorable view of socialism, compared to only 25 percent of Americans over age fifty-five.[9] When confronted with the actual definition of socialism, only 32 percent of millennials viewed it favorably.[10] It seems that those who desire the free promise of government more than the hard work required by free market capitalism tend to be those who haven't had to work much or for very long.

So, what should our biblical worldview be regarding hard work? How should we fight off the tendency toward materialism? Does God care about the person who has been disadvantaged?

---

9   Ekins and Pullmann, "Why So Many Millennials Are Socialists."
10 Ekins, "Opinion: Millennials like socialism—until they get jobs."

Hard Work

Consider 2 Thessalonians 3:6–12:

> Now we command you, brothers, in the name of our Lord Jesus Christ, that you keep away from any brother who is walking in idleness and not in accord with the tradition that you received from us. For you yourselves know how you ought to imitate us, because we were not idle when we were with you, nor did we eat anyone's bread without paying for it, but with toil and labor we worked night and day, that we might not be a burden to any of you. It was not because we do not have that right, but to give you in ourselves an example to imitate. For even when we were with you, we would give you this command: If anyone is not willing to work, let him not eat. For we hear that some among you walk in idleness, not as busy at work, but busybodies. Now such persons we command and encourage in the Lord Jesus Christ to do their work quietly and to earn their own living. (ESV)

The apostle Paul addressed issues of idleness in Thessalonica. The Thessalonians were focused on matters surrounding the end times, and false teachers were pointing followers of Christ in errant directions on matters of work, moral purity, and holy living. Paul, addressing many of these issues in his letters, deals with the matter of work as some, believing the day of the Lord to be imminent, had given themselves to idleness. Paul doesn't encourage them to live off the wealth of others. Instead, he admonishes them to follow his example of hard work to their great benefit. Paul goes on further to say, in 2 Thessalonians 3:10, "If anyone is not willing to work, let him not eat." Hard work is clearly not evil.

Materialism

What about the issue of materialism that some believe to be inherent in capitalism? What does the Bible have to say about this?

Look at Matthew 6:19–21: "Do not store up for yourselves treasures on earth, where moth and rust destroy, and where thieves break in and steal. But store up for yourselves treasures in heaven, where neither moth nor rust destroys, and where thieves do not break in or steal; for where your treasure is, there your heart will be also." The focus of the passage is not to avoid wealth but, rather, to treasure that which is most important—God himself. It's so often easy to get focused on the gift apart from the Giver. This is what is so abominable about the prosperity gospel movement. They seek to replace God with gifts. They seek to replace the gospel with goodies. The right and proper view of wealth is as a gift from the Master rather than an end in itself.

The Disadvantaged

Finally, what does the Bible say about those who have been disadvantaged?

God's Word from Old Testament to New Testament encourages the believer to be compassionate toward and generous to those in need. We would argue that America is the most generous nation in the world. Furthermore, we'd contend that those who believe in God are much more giving than those whose worldview denies his existence.

An article from *The Philanthropy Roundtable Almanac* called "Who Gives Most to Charity?" presented the following research findings:

> Among individual givers in the U.S., while the wealthy do their part, . . . the vast predominance of offerings come from average citizens of moderate income. Six out of ten U.S. households donate to charity in a given year, and the typical household's annual gifts add up to between two and three thousand dollars.
>
> *This is different from the patterns in any other country.* Per capita, Americans voluntarily donate about seven times as much as continental Europeans. Even our cousins the Canadians give to charity at substantially lower rates, and at half the total volume of an American household.
>
> There are many reasons for this American distinction. Foremost *is the fact that ours is the most religious nation in the industrial world. Religion motivates giving more than any other factor.* A second explanation is our deep-rooted tradition of mutual aid, which has impressed observers like Tocqueville since our founding days. Third is the potent entrepreneurial impulse in the U.S., which generates overflowing wealth that can be shared,

while simultaneously encouraging a "bootstrap" ethic that says we should help our neighbors pull themselves up.[11]

Ephesians 4:28 instructs us, "He who steals must steal no longer; but rather he must labor, performing with his own hands what is good, so that he will have something to share with one who has need." We often hear a justification for those who are down on their luck. We understand why they would break into a store and take what they need because they don't have enough. Except that's not how Scripture views this. Scripture instructs such a person to do honest work with his own hands.

The Generous Gospel

First John 3:17–18 says, "But whoever has the world's goods, and sees his brother in need and closes his heart against him, how does the love of God abide in him? Little children, let us not love with word or with tongue, but in deed and truth."

Here is an admonition and encouragement for those of us who love God to be giving. This giving isn't based on government compulsion but on the acknowledgement of what God has done on our behalf. It is grounded in the understanding that we are indeed sinners ourselves and owe a debt to God that we cannot repay. As a result of that debt, while we were unable, incapable, dead in sin and trespasses, the sovereign God of the universe sent his Son, Jesus Christ, to die a death he did not deserve on a Roman cross to redeem mankind. If we would just repent of our sin and place our full faith in Jesus Christ, we would inherit eternal life.

That's the gospel. That is what informed those who founded this nation. Flawed though they were, they understood the debt that was paid on behalf of sinners by a sovereign God and that individuals made in his image have inherent value and worth. The biblical worldview supports the tenets of capitalism, tenets based in morality, the foundation on which true freedom stands.

---

11 "Who Gives Most to Charity?" Philanthropy Roundtable, accessed June 14, 2021, https://www.philanthropyroundtable.org/almanac/statistics/who-gives, (emphasis added).

Discussion Questions

1. Based on this chapter, how is *capitalism* defined?
2. In our current culture, why is capitalism seen as evil?
3. What role does the doctrine of man play in understanding a capitalistic system?
4. What are the challenges of a capitalist system?
5. What are the benefits of a capitalist system?

A Social Savior

In the early 1990s, Shari Lewis, puppeteer and creator of the children's television show *Lamb Chop's Play-Along!*, popularized a song loathed by parents on cross-country road trips about a song that never ends. The song goes on in an infinite loop, cycling back into the same verse over and over, until an exasperated listener finally puts an end to it, perhaps using Lewis's strategy of a hand over the singer's mouth.

Much like "The Song That Doesn't End," today's conversations about justice seem to be caught in an endless playback loop. In his book *The Quest for Cosmic Justice*, Thomas Sowell highlights the problem: "Whatever moral principle each of us believes in, we call [that] justice, so we are only talking in a circle when we say that we advocate justice, unless we specify just what conception of justice we have in mind. This is especially so today, when so many advocate what they call 'social justice'— often with great passion, but with no definition."[1] Without an objective definition of the type of justice you have in mind, you're merely talking in a circle—and the circle just goes on and on, my friend.

---

1 Thomas Sowell, *The Quest for Cosmic Justice* (New York: Free Press, 2002), 3.

Without a definition established on an objective standard, we are left with our own subjective, morally relativistic standard of determining what is just. Current social justicians seem to wake up every day with a new set of standards, forming an ever-moving target of right and wrong, good and bad, moral and immoral. What was deemed moral, good, and right over the past one hundred years has now been determined to be flagrantly racist, bad, and immoral.

The Fallacy of Heaven on Earth

A problem many evangelical social justice advocates have today is that in their zeal to pursue "social justice" in the name of Christ, they too often confuse Christians with Christ, which is something that should never happen. As professor and church historian Thomas S. Kidd astutely said, "The Christian faith has only one perfect hero. He is our proper object, not just of emulation, but of worship. We all fall far, far short of his example."[2] Of course, the "one perfect hero" of whom Kidd is speaking is none other than Jesus Christ.

Not only do many evangelical social justicians expect Christians to be perfect as only Jesus was, which is what we mean by saying they have confused Christians with Christ, but they have also confused this unredeemed world with the redeemed world that Scripture clearly teaches is yet to come. In 2 Peter 3:13, the apostle Peter writes, "But according to His promise we [believers] are looking for new heavens and a new earth, in which righteousness dwells." In Isaiah 65:17, God himself declares, "For behold, I create new heavens and a new earth; and the former things will not be remembered or come to mind."

These passages are germane to our consideration of true justice because a fundamental fallacy of the social justice argument, particularly within evangelicalism, is that this "new heaven" and "new earth," which Scripture clearly teaches is an eschatological reality, can be brought to fruition in the here and now. We can experience this "heaven on earth," the argument goes, if only the church would

---

2 Thomas Kidd, "Slavery, Historical Heroes, and 'Precious Puritans,'" *Patheos*, October 9, 2012, https://www.patheos.com/blogs/anxiousbench/2012/10/historical-heroes-and-precious-puritans.

embrace what many evangelical social justicians believe is a mandate equal to that of heralding the gospel to a world that is perishing—namely, meeting people's felt needs.

A recent example of this kind of theological fallacy is a video of social and political activist Rev. William J. Barber II, who, among other roles, is president and senior lecturer of an organization called Repairers of the Breach and also serves as visiting professor at Union Theological Seminary in New York. In the video, Barber speaks at the summer 2019 meeting of the executive committee of the Democratic National Convention on behalf of The Poor People's Campaign: A National Call for Moral Revival. The stated purpose of his address was to "make the case for a national debate on systemic racism, poverty, ecological devastation, and the war economy."[3]

Barber argues for what he describes as an "interlocking focus" in order to build a "moral movement" to rid society of the aforementioned ills. Over the course of his speech, Barber cites and refers to the Bible on numerous occasions in an attempt to buttress his argument that not only the church but America as a nation must operate on the basis of a theonomistic sociopolitical worldview, one in which the law of God shapes and directs government policy. Barber is rather inconsistent, however, regarding how God's law, which is inherently objective, should be applied in society. On the one hand, he leverages the Scriptures in terms of how a nation like America should treat the poor while, on the other hand, totally disregards the principle of the *imago Dei* by supporting a woman's "right to choose" to murder her unborn child.

That Barber is pro-abortion is no surprise. The vast majority of liberal black Christians are as well. What is incredibly ironic is that Barber, in making a case for a woman's right to choose as a social justice issue, does so in front of a group whose political platform openly endorses the murder of unborn children who are created in the image of the same God in whom Barber professes to believe. The hypocrisy is breathtaking.

---

3 Rev. Dr. William J. Barber, II, "We Must Build a Moral Movement to Address Poverty," August 24, 2019, YouTube, https://youtu.be/dTsnCAMNxzE.

Listening to Barber speak of the "god" he worships—one that supports the murder of the unborn—it must be asked, "What god is this?" When we appeal to such subjective standards, we have to recognize that the god in view is the one we see in the mirror. And, of course, we are no gods at all. People like Barber have rejected the true God of the Bible and replaced him with themselves and whatever cause they support.

Social Justice Salvation

Barber's vision of heaven on earth doesn't end with a woman's right to choose. The goals and objectives of his Poor People's Campaign include demands for universal health care for all, fully funded social welfare programs that provide cash directly to the poor, and relief from wealth inequality.[4] According to Barber, the Bible supports these demands: "If someone calls it socialism, then we must compel them to acknowledge that the Bible also promotes socialism. Because Jesus offered free health care to everyone and never charged a leper a co-pay."[5]

Hermeneutical gymnastics notwithstanding, Barber actually had the temerity to pause in the midst of his remarks so he could revel in the naïve applause he received in response to his absurd and self-aggrandizing proclamation. It is a prime example of the sad reality—a sermon strong on homiletics may cause the average parishioner to ignore a proper hermeneutic. When a preacher is more a performer delivering a poem than a pastor with a prophetic voice calling men to repentance, he puts those in the audience back in the bondage of emotional slavery.

It is tragic to see the disadvantaged poor lap up this vile poison. When "reverends" like Barber preach heaven on earth through social justice, they only create more greed, rather than grace, and more hatred, rather than holiness, in those they engage. The number of things this poverty pimp posited, apart from any examination of facts,

---

[4] "Our Demands," The Poor People's Campaign, accessed October 10, 2020, https://www.poorpeoplescampaign.org/about/our-demands.
[5] Barber, "We Must Build."

was mind-blowing. He threw unexamined numbers and hypothetical solutions around as if they were salvific and able to create the utopian paradise only he could envision. Any question or self-reflection regarding the conditions that created the poverty to begin with were irrelevant to their existence. Someone else was always to blame.

Most importantly, Barber's assertion that the Bible promotes socialism is beyond the pale. Socialism clearly violates at least four of the Ten Commandments. It exchanges government for God, violating the first and second commandments. Socialism is theft and therefore violates the eighth commandment, which says, "You shalt not steal" (Exodus 20:15). Socialism also violates the tenth commandment by promoting covetousness among neighbors. How dare this so-called preacher use the Bible to advocate an economic system responsible for more poverty around the world than any other! He should be ashamed of himself, and those listening to him should rid him of his clerical vestments.

It doesn't take awfully long to realize that what Barber is advocating is not the gospel at all. Instead, he is championing a radical societal worldview that is more reflective of the principles of Marxism than the precepts of the biblical gospel of Jesus Christ.

What makes evangelical social justicians like Barber so dangerous is that what they propose is not merely an agenda to rid society of racism and poverty but an entirely new soteriology. Barber believes that social justice *is* salvation, not merely a by-product *of* salvation.

A Different Gospel

Men like Reverend Barber are evil. More than his poverty pimping or social justice soapboxing, Barber is presenting a different gospel. His soteriology is steeped in his own subjective ideas of societal change. For example, Barber claims that poverty in America is inhumane and demands that all people have a "right" to live differently in the wealthiest nation in the world. But we must ask, "By what standard does he define poverty?"

While people like Barber want to claim that racist policies are the cause for the vast majority of poverty in America, we would argue there's no other place in the world that anyone marching with Barber would rather be poor than in America. What it means to be poor in America is a status of tremendous wealth by any standard in any other country around the world. As evidenced by the hundreds of thousands of people every year risking their lives to enter America illegally, Barber's soteriological positions cannot stand the weight of scrutiny outside of the borders of the country he calls "wicked and racist." Barber's gospel of government salvation is insufficient to save.

In his letter to the church in Galatia, Paul delivers his strongest condemnation for those presenting a different gospel: "But even if we, or an angel from heaven should preach to you a gospel contrary to what we have preached to you, he is to be accursed. As we have said before, so I say again now, if any man is preaching to you a gospel contrary to the one you received, he is to be accursed!" (Galatians 1:8–9).

Judaizers in the region of Galatia were telling the churches that they needed to add something to the message of Paul and the gospel of Jesus. Barber outdoes the Judaizers by stripping the gospel of its good news about Jesus and replacing it with demanded actions of the government. This is a fundamental fallacy of the evangelical social justice movement, the eschatological view that the new heaven and new earth of which Scripture speaks can be made a reality by humanity in the present day. It is exactly what Barber and others who subscribe to his paradigm of social justice believe.

This eschatological worldview is what James Cone, the father of black liberation theology, referred to as "creative discipleship." As Cone writes in his book *Black Theology & Black Power*,

> With a black perspective, eschatology comes to mean joining the world and making it what it ought to be. It means that the Christian man looks to the future not for a reward or possible punishment of evildoers, but as a means of making him dissatisfied with the present. His only purpose for looking to a distant past or an unrealized future is that both disclose the ungodliness of

the present. Looking to the future he sees that present injustice cannot be tolerated. Black Theology asserts an eschatology that confronts a world of racism with Black Power. Eschatology does not mean merely salvation of the soul, individual rescue from the evil world, comfort for the troubled conscience, but also the realization of the eschatological hope of justice, the humanizing of man, the socializing of humanity, and peace for all creation.[6]

Cone explains perfectly the current day "gospel of grievance," which is the consistent theme of the social justician. It seems that every day brings a new grievance, something new over which to be outraged. Interestingly enough, if there isn't anything today to be upset about, social justicians will look into the past for something (*anything*) that they can celebrate as a new grievance. Their eschatological view does not include a future hope but rather a future *pain* that will be suffered today apart from some action on their part to change society. Barber and Cone share this eschatology, believing humanity can save itself and by human efforts bring the kingdom of God on earth, particularly through a partnership of church and state.

This kind of paternalistic partnership between the church and the state is a fundamental reason why the social gospel is not the biblical gospel. Contrary to what is taught in Scripture, the social gospel promotes the idea that humanity has the inherent capacity and desire to accomplish within society what can only be done in the human heart through the work of the Holy Spirit.

Evangelical social justicians like Reverend Barber would do well to consider what Ronald H. Nash writes in his book *Social Justice and the Christian Church*:

> The liberal's obsession with the proper distribution of society's goods binds him to a crucial truth: that before society can have enough to distribute among the needy, a sufficient quantity of goods must be produced. By focusing all their attention on who gets what, defenders of the welfare state promote policies that severely restrict production. Advocates of the welfare state paint a picture of an unending flow of cash from the producers

---

6 James Cone, *Black Theology & Black Power* (Maryknoll, NY: Orbis, 1997), 126.

in society to the non-producers. But as the sphere of benefits for the non-productive segment of society continues to increase, the mass of marginal producers realizes that the gap between them and welfare recipients is shrinking. Inevitably, they begin to lose their incentive to continue as producers—and as taxpayers. So they give up and join the ever-growing army drawing welfare benefits paid for by the diminishing group of producers. Liberal social policies that continue to drain a society's productive capacities hold ominous implications for the welfare of future generations.[7]

A "Moral Movement"

The genesis of all injustice and unrighteousness in the world is sin—the solution to which is not more laws or government austerity but that people would come to faith in Jesus Christ and live lives of obedience to him. Why would Barber, or any other professing Christian, expect a society that hates God to conduct itself as if it loves him? In his Poor People's Campaign speech, Barber declares repeatedly that America is in need of a "moral movement" to address issues like poverty, racism, and injustice, and he leverages the Bible as the authority on which that moral movement should be organized and carried out. But there is something inherently problematic with positing Scripture as merely a moral authority.

John MacArthur deals with this kind of "moralistic soteriology" in his book *Christ's Call to Reform the Church*:

> People can change their lives. They can have a moment of crisis and decide they're going to turn away from immorality or addiction and start living a better life. People can, to some degree, clean up their act simply by applying extraordinary human effort and resolve. If enough of them do it, there can be a slight moral upgrade in human society. But behavioral reform has no bearing on people's relationship with God. It has no means to deliver them out of the bondage of sin into the kingdom of Christ. The best that morality can do is turn people into another batch of condemned

---

7 Ronald Nash, *Social Justice and the Christian Church* (Lima, OH: Academic Renewal Press, 2002), 89.

Pharisees. Morality can't save anyone from guilt or fuel genuine godliness. Pharisees and prostitutes share the same hell. . . .

Neither social change nor moralism were ever the message of the Old Testament prophets. They were never the message of the Messiah or the New Testament writers. Such has never been God's message to the world at all. In fact, Isaiah tells us that "all our righteous deeds are like a filthy garment" (Isaiah 64:6). Man's morality at its apex is nothing more than foul, defiled rags.[8]

Theologian John Frame agrees, writing in his *Systematic Theology*, "As a dead man cannot get up and walk around, so a morally dead person cannot do works pleasing to God. The sinful nature is not something we acquired during our lifetime. It is ours from birth, even from conception. So we cannot prevent it any more than we can do away with it in our own strength."[9]

The person who would confuse behavioral moralism with spiritual regeneration is facing a theological conundrum because the reality is that the Qur'an is full of moral precepts as well. So are the Vedas in Hinduism, the Tripitaka or the "Three Baskets" in Buddhism, the Book of Mormon in Mormonism, and the Zend Avesta in Zoroastrianism. With that being the case, we would ask Reverend Barber, "Why should society accept the Bible as the sole authority upon which his 'moral movement' should be constructed?" After all, if the solution to the ills of society is merely that human beings need to be "better" or "more moral" toward one another, why bother subscribing to the Bible's construct of morality and justice? Why not subscribe to one of the many other religious pathways as being equally valid and efficacious? Here's why: because none of those other pathways is rooted in the truth, and nothing that is grounded in falsehood can ever be accepted as authoritative.

Only truth is authoritative. And truth is found only in the Word of God. As Jesus prayed in John 17:17, "Sanctify them in the truth; Your word *is* truth" (emphasis added).

---

8 John MacArthur, *Christ's Call to Reform the Church* (Chicago: Moody, 2018), 11.
9 John Frame, *Systematic Theology: An Introduction to Christian Belief* (Phillipsburg, NJ: P&R, 2013), 860.

The appeal of moralistic therapeutic deism is real, and we're afraid that these men have completely ignored the God of the Bible and replaced him with a god of their own making. The morality to which they appeal looks nothing like the regeneration-based moral code found in Scripture. Barber's morality doesn't include the sanctity of human life, the honoring of marriage between one man and one woman, or a call for the centrality of the gospel of Jesus Christ for salvation. Barber's god is government, and that god will always fail.

Christians, Not Statists

Reverend Barber tacitly claimed that the Bible supports socialism. But how can the eternal Word of God support a worldly philosophy that has only existed since the late eighteenth century?

It should go without saying that, as believers in Jesus Christ, the only true God, each of us should do what we can with the resources he blesses us with and the opportunities he provides us to help those who are legitimately in need. But even so, there is a biblical precept involved in carrying out that mandate, and it is found in Galatians 6:10. There the apostle Paul states, "So then, while we have opportunity, let us do good to all people, and especially those who are of the household of the faith."

As the body of Christ seeks to meet pressing needs in society, the biblical precept is that we do so from the inside out—that is, meet needs within the church first and then those in the world, not the other way around. And the resources for meeting those needs should come from within the church itself, not from government. The reality is that we are Christians; we are not statists. As John the Baptist declares in John 3:27, "A man can receive nothing unless it has been given him from heaven." He did not say that "a man can receive nothing unless it has been given him by the state."

Social justicians like Reverend Barber are propagating the myth that it is entirely possible to eliminate poverty completely from society. But as Jesus said in Matthew 26:11, "The poor you will always have with you" (NIV). The word "poor" in that text is the Greek noun *ptochos*, which denotes those who are destitute of wealth, influence, position, or power, those who are afflicted and helpless. The word "always" is the Greek adverb *pantote*, which means "at all times." According to Jesus, there will never be a time in this present world and society where there will not be those who are poor or oppressed—*never*.

A Message, Not a Movement

What quasi-Christian social justicians like Reverend Barber fail to understand is that Jesus was not a community organizer. As such, his church is not to be viewed or regarded as a political action committee.

Jesus's earthly ministry was conducted amid one of the most ruthless and oppressive regimes in human history—the Roman government under Caesar Augustus. Yet never once during the three and a half years of His earthly ministry did Jesus command his followers to protest, demonstrate, or remonstrate against the perceived injustices of the Roman government. Yes, people did protest during that time, but Jesus never commanded *his* followers to do so. The gospel of Jesus Christ is a message, not a movement. It is a proclamation, not a political platform.

Jesus declared in John 18:36 that "My kingdom is not of this world. If My kingdom were of this world, then My servants would be fighting so that I would not be handed over to the Jews; but as it is, My kingdom is not of this realm." The word "fighting" in that text is the Greek verb *agōnizomai*, which translated means "to contend with adversaries in order to obtain something." Nowhere in the New Testament is the church told to fight for anything or to organize "poor people's marches" or to align itself with any political entity or organization. Jesus said his servants would fight *if* his kingdom were of this world, but it is not. Why is that so hard for the church to understand? Why are people like Reverend Barber acting as if the kingdom of God is of this world when Jesus himself clearly said it is not?

In Romans 8:22, Paul said, "For we know that the whole creation groans and suffers the pains of childbirth together until now." Paul is referring metaphorically to Genesis 3:16 and the consequences that fell not only on Adam and Eve and their progeny—namely, you and me—but on creation *itself* because of sin. Sin is the mortal enemy of society, not poverty, not homelessness, and not injustice. All those things are merely manifestations of the kind of "groaning" and "suffering" that Paul is talking about in Romans 8. And as we have clearly established in this chapter, Scripture is unambiguous about the fact that groaning and suffering will never cease to be a reality in this world until Christ returns to make all things new.

God's Word says in Deuteronomy 15:11, "For the poor will never cease to be in the land; therefore I command you, saying, 'You shall freely open your hand to your brother, to your needy and poor in your land.'" Now, undoubtedly, someone reading that is going to see the second half of that verse and respond, "See! The Bible does teach social justice!" No, friend. When you and I do as that text says, when we open our hand to our brother and to the needy and poor in the land, the Bible calls that obedience, not "social justice."

The gospel of Jesus Christ is not a movement. It's a message of salvation for sinners. It's those preaching a different gospel who have decided to craft their own movement. And in changing the message of the gospel, they seek a savior that cannot save.

A Savior for Sinners, Not Society

Jesus Christ came into this world to save sinners, not society. This is why he was given the name *Jesus* to begin with. Matthew 1:21 explains, "[Mary] will bear a Son; and you shall call His name Jesus, for He will save His people from their sins."

The primary role of the church is to proclaim to lost sinners the exact same message Jesus pronounced: "Repent and believe in the gospel" (Mark 1:15). That is the core mission and purpose of the church in the world today.

As D. Martyn Lloyd-Jones writes in his book *Great Doctrines of the Bible*, "they say that what we call sin is merely the absence of certain qualities. You must not say a man is positively bad; what you mean is that he is not good; sin is negative. But the Bible says that sin is positive. It is not the absence of goodness, it is the positive presence of evil and of badness. And that is something which we must emphasize because from the very beginning it is emphasized, constantly, in the Scriptures themselves."[10]

If you're looking to Jesus as some kind of "social savior," you need to reassess your Christology because that's not the Jesus of the Bible. What society needs is salvation from sin. That is why Jesus came into the world—to set free those who are captive to sin (Luke 4:18). Salvation from our sin is the salvation Scripture declares to the world, not the moralistic therapeutic deism propagated by evangelical social justicians like Reverend William Barber.

As we saw in 2 Peter 3:13, Christ has promised a new heaven and a new earth in which his righteousness will dwell forever. This righteousness is not the man-centered, politically manufactured righteousness of Reverend Barber. It is a righteousness that flows from the innately pure and indefectible character of God himself.

In Revelation 22:11, Christ says, "Let the one who does wrong, still do wrong; and the one who is filthy, still be filthy." In other words, until Christ returns to earth to make all things new, the ills and injustices of society will continue to be. They cannot be protested or legislated away. The only hope for the church, and the world, is Jesus Christ and him crucified.

Why does the church act as if politics were the answer to the problems of the world? The problem of the world is sin, not who is president or prime minister or king. When will the church get it through its collective thick skull that saviors aren't elected? When injustice occurs, we must look to Christ, the righteous One who rules and reigns over all creation, not to some elected official or political party with no power over the attitudes of the human heart. We must pay attention to the warnings of Scripture.

- "If you see oppression of the poor and denial of justice and righteousness in the province, do not be shocked at the sight; for one official watches over another official, and there are higher officials over them" (Ecclesiastes 5:8)

---

10 D. Martyn Lloyd-Jones, *Great Doctrines of the Bible* (Wheaton, IL: Crossway, 2012), 201.

- "It is better to take refuge in the Lord than to trust in man. It is better to take refuge in the Lord than to trust in princes" (Psalm 118:8–9).
- "Do not trust in princes, in mortal man, in whom there is no salvation. His spirit departs, he returns to the earth; in that very day his thoughts perish" (Psalm 146:3–4).

Jesus Christ is not a socialist. He is the Savior. The sooner the church realizes this, the better it and society will be.

Discussion Questions

1. What is the problem the social justician believes needs solving?
2. Those holding the idea of socialist savior have a particular eschatology. What are they trying to create?
3. How does 2 Peter 3:13 respond to the social justician?
4. According to this chapter, what is the different gospel being preached by the social justician?
5. The gospel is a message, not a movement. Why is that distinction important when everything seems to be a "gospel issue"?

The Born-Alive Act

America is thoroughly and unarguably a *post-Christian* nation. By this, we mean that America as a society no longer views the Word of God as its primary guide for defining objectively the social, cultural, and political standards by which we, as its citizens, are to live. There was once a time when that was so—hence the term "*post*-Christian." But it is clear, by much contemporary evidence, that this is no longer the case and has not been for quite some time.

One of the evidences to which we are alluding is the recent failure by the United States Senate to pass Senate Bill 311, the Born-Alive Abortion Survivors Protection Act. More commonly referred to as the "Born-Alive Act," the bill was introduced by Nebraska Senator Ben Sasse, a Republican, on January 31, 2019. The Born-Alive Act was intended to accomplish two primary things legislatively:

1. If an abortion results in the live birth of an infant, the infant is a legal person for all purposes under the laws of the United States, and entitled to all the protections of such laws.

2. Any infant born alive after an abortion or within a hospital, clinic, or other facility has the same claim to the protection of the law that would arise for any newborn, or for any person who comes to a hospital, clinic, or other facility for

screening and treatment or otherwise becomes a patient within its care.[1]

These were the two pillars on which the Born-Alive Act rested. We say "were," past tense, because on February 25 of both 2019 and 2020, the proposed legislation failed to achieve the necessary votes to move forward in the United States Senate. In the most recent 2020 vote, all fifty-three Republican senators voted in favor of the act, and forty of the forty-five Democrat senators voted against it.[2]

Now, notwithstanding the tragic reality that the Born-Alive Act failed to pass, what we want to focus on in this chapter is not *that* the legislation failed to pass but *why* it failed to pass. The reasons are not political but theological in nature.

A Theological Issue

It is essential for us to understand this difference, not only in the discussion of this bill but about abortion altogether. We tend to couch this discussion merely in terms of political rhetoric, and while this does have political implications, the genesis of the issue is theological. We are dealing with the *imago Dei*, the image of God, and how we think about abortion is directly related to what we think of God and what he decrees. If we understand that, all our political discussion stops, and we must pause and look at what God says.

This issue also has much to do with how we view ourselves. The people who do not care about this act and its purpose in saving the lives of babies born alive are the same people who don't believe they are being described in Ecclesiastes 9:3, where the author writes, "This is an evil in all that is done under the sun, that there is one fate for all men. Furthermore, the hearts of the sons of men are full of evil and insanity is in their hearts throughout their lives." The hearts of those who support the practice of abortion are full of evil and insanity.

---

[1] Born-Alive Abortion Survivors Protection Act, S. 311, 116th Cong. (2019).
[2] "All Actions S.311—116th Congress (2019-2020)," Congress.gov, https://www.congress.gov/bill/116th-congress/senate-bill/311/all-actions?overview=closed&q=%7B%22roll-call-vote%22%3A%22all%22%7D.

To get down to the root causes of why this bill failed, we must look at this issue from a biblical context, starting with the writing of the apostle James: "Who among you is wise and understanding? Let him show by his good behavior his deeds in the gentleness of wisdom. But if you have bitter jealousy and selfish ambition in your heart, do not be arrogant and so lie against the truth. This wisdom [arrogance and lying] is not that which comes down from above, but is earthly, natural, demonic. For where jealousy and selfish ambition exist, there is disorder and every evil thing" (James 3:13–16). In this passage James gives us the reasons why the Born-Alive Act failed to pass. It is because of arrogant and selfish ambition that is earthly, worldly, and demonic.

We would be mistaken to think it is solely the fault of a group of elected politicians that this bill failed to pass. The sad reality is that much of the blame must be placed with Christians. The fact is that many of the politicians who voted against the Born-Alive Act are in office in the first place because of our own earthly, natural, and demonic arrogance that helped put them there.

Missing: A Biblical Worldview

This reality is a result of the fact that the vast majority of Christians in America don't possess a biblical worldview. We would even venture to suggest that were we to poll a group of professing Christians "on the street," so to speak, and ask them to articulate what their worldview was, many of them would not know what the word *worldview* meant, let alone what their worldview actually was.

In his book *Culture: Living as Citizens of Heaven on Earth*, A. W. Tozer writes, "A right view of God and the world to come requires that we have a right view of the world in which we live and our relation to it."[3] That's a great definition of a worldview. Tozer continues, "So much depends on this that we cannot afford to be careless about it." It is as if Tozer knew there would be some issues of worldview that Christians wouldn't care about. Even as we write, our hearts

---

3 A. W. Tozer, *Culture: Living as Citizens of Heaven on Earth* (Chicago: Moody, 2016), 118.

are burdened by the vast numbers of Christians in our country who probably don't care at all about the issue of abortion. They lack a biblical worldview.

One of the areas of American society in which this absence of a biblical worldview is most apparent is politics. Too many Christians today are comfortable supporting candidates for office through the lens of what the apostle James described as wisdom that is selfish, earthly, natural, and demonic. Their support of these candidates is grounded in how electing a certain individual to office will benefit them, all the while not caring about what the candidates' worldview or philosophy of life is or the paradigm of ethics and morality that guides them.

That the Born-Alive Act failed to pass the Senate is as much the responsibility of Christians who helped elect many of these politicians to office as it is the politicians themselves who voted against it. It is a reality that begs the question of those who profess to be followers of Jesus Christ: what worldview guides you when you step into the voting booth? Is it a conviction about the all-encompassing veracity of Scripture, or the earthly and arrogant wisdom of self? Which do you take into the voting booth with you?

The reality is that Christianity has answers to every issue of life. We can open the Bible and deal with anything that comes. But we are involved in a consumeristic Christianity where many of us are content to sit back and listen to a sermon or class but never taking notes, never taking responsibility on our own shoulders to learn things for ourselves and then to pass it on to the next generation.

Additionally, what we are learning should affect us in such a way that, as we live our lives, we are expanding the impact of the kingdom. We must go to the pages of Scripture and, rather than leaving the text in the first century, look at things as they are and then consider how we are to apply and leverage those things today. For example, in the first verse of the third chapter of Galatians, Paul asks his readers, "Who has bewitched you?" as he points out their error in believing that salvation could come through works of the law rather than by grace through faith. This isn't just an early church problem. According to Pew Research, 52 percent of American Protestant Christians believe that salvation is by grace and works.[4] What does this tell us? We've not been informed about our faith but have left it in the pages of Scripture, never applying it purposely to our own lives where it has implications for how we vote and think about laws, where we attend school or work, and how we interact with the people in our lives. As believers, we must realize that we have a living faith that has implications and applications for our modern lives. That realization is foundational to a biblical worldview.

Human Autonomy

The importance and significance of Christians having a biblical worldview—not only when it comes to politics but to all aspects of life—is captured very well in Daniel J. Mahoney's book entitled *The Idol of Our Age: How the Religion of Humanity Subverts Christianity*. In the chapter on "The Humanitarian Ethos," Mahoney writes this:

> Moral cognition is deepened and enriched by a truly substantial account of the moral life and the human soul. Without a religious appreciation of the full range of human needs—and not the cacophony of human wants posited by humanitarian materialism—the spiritual dimensions of human life are all but forgotten. Additionally, religion in general, and Christianity in particular, has a unique capacity to reconcile "personal freedom, dignity, selfhood and vitality with social discipline and coordination." The Christian cannot imagine the safeguarding of the morés of society without the surviving of a vigorous and demanding religious sensibility. Religion helps to make human beings and societies "whole," to reconcile the sacred and the mundane, the freedom of persons and the requirements of civilized order. Without religion, and in the West that means biblical religion, the person becomes a mere individual and society loses the capacity for a common good and the kind of collective action that respects the moral integrity of human

---

4 "U.S. Protestants Are Not Defined by Reformation-Era Controversies 500 Years Later," Pew Research Center, August 31, 2017, https://www.pewforum.org/2017/08/31/u-s-protestants-are-not-defined-by-reformation-era-controversies-500-years-later.

beings. The Christian notion of the person affirms human liberty and dignity while avoiding the illusion of human autonomy.[5]

Consider that final sentence, "The Christian notion of the person affirms human liberty and dignity while avoiding the illusion of human autonomy." What Mahoney says here is crucial because, when all has been said and done, abortion is about one thing and only one thing: human autonomy.

To believe in human autonomy is to live in the same paradigm as the Scriptures declare in Job 21:14, "They say to God, 'Depart from us! We do not even desire the knowledge of your ways.'" Those who accept the illusion of human autonomy are essentially telling God, "Leave us alone! We don't even desire to know Your ways, much less obey your ways." There is a word for the kind of defiant mindset that Job is talking about. It's called *humanism*.

Living without God

What exactly is humanism? Well, according to the American Humanist Association (AHA), humanism is defined as "a progressive philosophy of life that, without theism or other supernatural beliefs, affirms our ability and responsibility to lead ethical lives of personal fulfillment that aspire to the greater good."[6]

Did you catch that one phrase, "without theism"? That is, without God or any notion *of* God. In other words, it's exactly as Job said: "Depart from us, God! We do not even desire the knowledge of Your ways."

When you listen to statements made by advocates of abortion and abortion rights, their desire to reason without God is clear. A phrase often heard is "I think the woman should make the decision. I think the woman has the right to choose." This is an echo of the same human autonomy and humanism found in Genesis 3. Satan comes in and deceives the woman, asking, "Did God really say?" This is the

---
5 Daniel J. Mahoney, *The Idol of Our Age: How the Religion of Humanity Subverts Christianity* (New York: Encounter Books, 2020), 69–70.
6 "Definition of Humanism," American Humanist Association, accessed December 18, 2020, https://americanhumanist.org/what-is-humanism/definition-of-humanism.

question of all questions; challenging God, usurping God's authority, and determining to do what God said ought not to be done. We must not approach the issue of abortion this way. It must be considered in theological terms. Instead, we've taken it out of the pages of Scripture and into the halls of politics. That is not where it belongs. It must be anchored in our understanding of what Scripture has to say about this issue.

When you stop to think critically about the definition of humanism as proffered by the AHA, you have to ask yourself, Have you ever heard such hypocritical drivel in your life? They state that their worldview "affirms our ability and responsibility to lead ethical lives of personal fulfillment that aspire to the greater good" but "without theism"—without God.

Seriously? Without theism, where does this so-called responsibility to lead ethical lives come from in terms of an objective standard of morality? There isn't a standard at all. The individual basically becomes his own god. And is there not an inherent contradiction between the idea of living a life of "personal fulfillment" and aspiring to the "greater good"? In other words, if the focus is primarily on the *self*, how can that possibly lead to a greater good for others? This is the logic that abortion proponents try to follow, the pursuit of human autonomy and a life lived apart from God.

This way of thinking is totally contrary to the Scriptural imperative we have in Philippians 2:3-4, where Paul writes, "Do nothing from selfishness or empty conceit, but with humility of mind regard one another as more important than yourselves; do not merely look out for your own personal interests, but also for the interests of others." What we have in this passage is Paul giving us a great definition of what our lives should be about, not caught up in our own autonomy and our desire to do our own thing but submitted to the will of God. Paul goes on in the text to give the fullest example of what this should look like in the example of Christ. The God-man comes on the scene, and Paul writes, "Have this attitude in yourselves which was also in Christ Jesus, who, although He existed in the form of God, did not regard equality with God a thing to be grasped, but emptied Himself by taking the form of a bond-servant, and being made in the likeness of men. Being found in appearance as a man, He humbled Himself by becoming obedient to the point of death, even death on a cross" (vv. 5–8).

We have naturally exalted ourselves above God, but here we have the right example we are to model our lives after: Christ, who being in the form of God humbled himself even to the point of death. That we shake our fists angrily at God in an attempt to do what we desire exposes the wickedness of mankind. We're going to tell God what human life is. We're going to tell God what we want to do. This is the very core of human autonomy, and it traces back to original sin (Romans 5:12).

Humanism's Twisted Reasoning

Listen to what Louis Berkhof, in his *Systematic Theology*, has to say about the kind of twisted reasoning inherent in humanism:

> There is a certain liberty that is the inalienable possession of a free agent, namely, the liberty to choose as he pleases, in full accord with the prevailing dispositions and tendencies of his soul. *Man did not lose* any of the constitutional faculties necessary to constitute him a responsible moral agent. He still has the reason, conscience, and the freedom of choice. He has the ability to acquire knowledge, and to feel and recognize moral distinctions and obligations; and his affections, tendencies, and actions are spontaneous, so that he chooses many things that are good and amiable, benevolent and just, in the relations he sustains to his fellow-beings. *But man did lose* his material freedom, that is, the rational power to determine his course in the direction of the highest good, in harmony with the original moral constitution of his nature. Man has by nature an irresistible bias for evil. He is not able to apprehend and love spiritual excellence, to seek and do spiritual things, the things of God that pertain to salvation.[7]

Contrary to what the AHA says in their definition of humanism, that man has the ability to pursue the highest good, Berkhof argues that man has lost the rational power to do so and, in fact, has "an

---

7 Louis Berkhof, *Systematic Theology* (Louisville, KY: GLH, 2017), 204.

irresistible bias for evil." Recall Ecclesiastes 9:3, "The hearts of the sons of men are full of evil and insanity is in their hearts throughout their lives."

Berkhof has captured the essence of what the apostle Paul says in 1 Corinthians 2:12–14, which stands in direct contradiction to the claim of humanism: "Now we have received, not the spirit of the world, but the Spirit who is from God, so that we may know the things freely given to us by God, which things we also speak, not in words taught by human wisdom, but in those taught by the Spirit, combining spiritual thoughts with spiritual words. *But a natural man does not accept the things of the Spirit of God, for they are foolishness to him; and he cannot understand them, because they are spiritually appraised*" (emphasis added).

So, antithetical to the philosophical worldview promoted by the American Humanist Association, both Berkhof and Paul declare, "No, humanists, you're wrong. Mankind is wholly incapable of aspiring to the 'highest good.'" Consider Ecclesiastes 7:20, which says, "Indeed, there is not a righteous man on earth who continually does good and who never sins." Not only are we incapable of aspiring to the highest good, but Scripture teaches that we naturally do the exact opposite. Genesis 6:5 is just one example: "Then the LORD saw that the wickedness of man was great on the earth, and that every intent of the thoughts of his heart was only evil continually." Without God, we don't possess the ability to pursue good.

Questions for Humanism

Reflecting on the worldview of the AHA through the lens of Scripture raises some questions:

- What is the "greater good"? What is the genesis of it as an idea? How is the term *greater good* objectively defined?
- If you aspire to live a life "without theism," then why aspire to the greater good to begin with if there is no God to whom you'll be accountable and from whom you'll be rewarded for doing so? Why not aspire to the "greater evil"? Better yet, why aspire to any moral or ethical standard at all? Why not

just embrace nihilism, which is based on the ethos "eat and drink, for tomorrow we die," and just be done with it?

Humanism is fraught with theological and philosophical problems. Its shallowness is perhaps best described in the words of, ironically, a humanist—in this case, Kurt Vonnegut, the AHA's 1994 Humanist of the Year and a past honorary president of that organization. Vonnegut said this: "I am a humanist, which means, in part, that I have tried to behave decently without rewards or punishment after I am dead."[8]

What an utterly fatalistic and confusing worldview to have. If you are convinced there is no God, why are you concerned with living decently without rewards after you are dead? Why does that concept even cross your mind? Why try to behave decently if your entire worldview is based on living a life without theism? What does "decently" even mean, based on a standard that doesn't include God?

Even in the wording of this statement you can see that Vonnegut doesn't believe he can actually behave decently, only that he has "tried" to do so. Whatever standard he has placed, even in his own mind, is not achievable. This should tell him there is something beyond himself he is accountable to, a standard that God says is written on his heart through natural revelation (Romans 1:20). But Vonnegut would certainly not acknowledge that.

A Depraved Mind

This is the mindset of those who wish to live a life of human autonomy—apart from God—and who have absolutely no desire to know the ways of God. It's Romans 1 all day long: "For the wrath of God is revealed from heaven against all ungodliness and unrighteousness of men who suppress the truth in unrighteousness, because that which is known about God is evident within them, for God made it evident to them" (Romans 1:18–19). This is where you get your idea of decency, of living a good life, of aspiring to the greater good, Mr. Vonnegut. God has written it on your heart. You just refuse to acknowledge it—which leads us right to the rest of Romans 1: "And just as they did not see fit

---

8 "Famous Humanists in History," American Humanist Association, accessed December 18, 2020, https://americanhumanist.org/what-is-humanism/famous-humanists-in-history.

to acknowledge God any longer, God gave them over to a depraved mind to do those things which are not proper, . . . and although they know the ordinance of God, that those who practice such things are worthy of death, they not only do the same, but also give hearty approval to those who practice them" (vv. 28, 32).

That the Born-Alive Act would fail to be passed is a glaring example of the kind of "depraved mind" Paul is talking about in Romans 1. The adjective *depraved* in the Greek denotes a mind that is totally degenerate, corrupt, and unprincipled. Matthew Henry, in his commentary on Romans 1, described this "depraved mind" as a "blind, seared conscience, having lost all sensitivity to sin."[9] This is the kind of mind that applauds a society being able to legally murder children even after they've been born.

What kind of rational, reasonable thought process is being used to promote the idea that it is morally correct to have the option to kill a baby born alive? What are our elected officials thinking? How are they defending this? The typical, tired rationale is that a woman should have the right to choose. But some have argued that because a child so rarely survives an abortion, there is no need for the Born-Alive Act. Yet the rarity of other crimes hasn't impacted the consideration of other bills. Consider, for example, the Antilynching Act, passed by the House of Representatives in recent months.[10] Regardless of how liberal the definition of *lynching*, its frequency falls far below that of children who survive abortion, yet amplifying penalties for those who participate in lynching was celebrated, while protecting the personhood of the just-born was disregarded as unnecessary.

This is such flawed thinking and evidence of a seared conscience. Those who reason this way have no sensitivity to the fact that sin is at work within them. Evil and insanity are in their hearts. Tragically, some who believe this call themselves Christians, and Christians are helping elect them to political office.

---

9   Matthew Henry, *The New Matthew Henry Commentary: the Classic Work with Updated Language*, ed. Martin H. Manser (Grand Rapids: Zondervan, 2010), 2011.
10   Emmett Till Antilynching Act, H.R. 35, 116th Cong. (2019).

Fundamentally, the Born-Alive Act failed to pass for reasons that are theological, not political. Notwithstanding the failure of the act to pass in the Senate, much of the fault lies at the feet of Christians who are inclined to apply the principles found in God's Word to only certain areas of their lives and not others. In fact, if more professing Christians held to an all-encompassing biblical worldview, perhaps we wouldn't be having this conversation. But here we are.

Worldview Matters

The Born-Alive Act, like every other area of life, must be viewed in the light of Scripture. It is this very necessity of an all-encompassing biblical worldview that Wayne Grudem addresses in his book *Politics According to the Bible*. Grudem writes,

> A Christian worldview must include the idea that there is a measure of moral evil in the heart of every human being who lives on the face of the earth. In addition, the Bible shows that this moral evil in human beings must be defined in comparison to an external standard of right and wrong, a standard that comes not from the human race but from God himself. This one idea, that human beings are viewed as sinful before the absolute moral standards of the one true God, has immense implications for numerous policy differences between Republicans and Democrats.[11]

Grudem nails it. To have or not have a biblical worldview has immense implications, and the defeat of the Born-Alive Act is one of those implications. When Christians do not take a biblical worldview with them into the voting booth, we help put the politicians in place who vote down a bill to keep a born baby alive. Christians are at fault here.

Our minds must be captive to the Word of God and our entire intellectual structure shaped and determined by biblical truth. We who claim the name of Jesus Christ have no excuse not to have an

---

11 Wayne Grudem, *Politics According to the Bible: A Comprehensive Resource for Understanding Modern Political Issues in Light of Scripture* (Grand Rapids: Zondervan, 2010), 119.

all-encompassing biblical worldview of life. We cannot subjectively pick and choose where we will apply the Word of God and where we will not.

In his *Institutes of the Christian Religion*, John Calvin writes, "The obedience which we have taught is owed to superiors must always allow for an exception, or rather for a rule which is to be observed above everything else."[12] If this is applied to the contemporary topic of the Born-Alive Act, we may ask, "Christian, do you have a rule that you will not vote for a candidate who supports killing babies—period? Is that a rule you live by above everything else when you consider who to support during an election?"

Calvin continues, "Such obedience should not deflect us from obedience to him with whose will all that kings desire should rightly comply." In other words, as we consider the Born-Alive Act, if a candidate's position on the *imago Dei* nature of unborn babies, or in this case, born babies, does not comply with the will of God, they don't get our vote. Returning to Calvin, we read, "With whose will all that kings desire should rightly comply, to whose ordinance all their commands should yield, and by whose majesty all their arrogance should be humbled and abased."[13] Recall that James 3 defines wisdom that is not from God as earthly, natural, and demonic, full of arrogance and lies (James 3:13–18). Calvin uses that same word, *arrogance*, here.

Calvin concludes, "And in truth, how willful would it be if, to satisfy men, we incurred the anger of him for whose sake we obey men? The Lord is thus the King of kings who, as soon as he opens his sacred mouth, must be heard above all men, for all men, and before all men."[14] What better time to remember Calvin's words than when we are discerning for whom we should cast our vote? We must be aware that all these politicians will one day bow the knee before Jesus Christ, as will each of us. We will be held accountable, even for how we voted.

---

12 John Calvin, *Institutes of the Christian Religion*, 4.20.32.
13 Calvin, 4.20.32.
14 Calvin, 4.20.32.

A good friend of ours, Summer White Jaeger, the host of the *Sheologians* podcast, understands the impact that a biblical worldview has on all of life. "As believers," she writes, "we must live as though God has spoken & it has real-time effect in our lives. God has defined sin, justice, manhood, womanhood, goodness, and righteousness. We must act accordingly."[15] God has chosen us before the foundation of the world, not only for eternity but also to obey him right now, in real time.

Politics Is Theology

Politics *is* theology. Politics is not something Christians can partition off or treat as separate from how we view any other aspect of our existence as followers of Christ in this nation. We cannot segregate how we apply the Bible in our lives. The Word of God either applies to all of life or to none of it. It is not a buffet for us to walk through, taking what we like and leaving the rest. Instead, we are to be salt and light in the world (Matthew 5:13–16). When you salt a dish, do you keep the salt on just part of it, or do you salt the whole thing? Any cook would tell you the salt must permeate the entire dish because you want the whole thing to taste like it is seasoned. Yet some Christians miss this point, adding the salt of the gospel to just some parts of their lives. No! We are to be salt and light to the whole world, and that means we must have a biblical worldview that applies to every single area of life.

Christians must begin to scrutinize political candidates against the objective truth of the Word of God and, consequently, cast our votes for those candidates within the framework of an objective biblical worldview and not as autonomous human beings. As the apostle Paul writes, "Or do you not know that your body is a temple of the Holy Spirit who is in you, whom you have from God, and that you are not your own? For you have been bought with a price" (1 Corinthians 6:19–20).

We are indeed living in a post-Christian society. There is no doubt about that. In discarding God's Word as our moral compass, we have convinced ourselves that God will not judge us and that we are

---

15 Summer Jaeger, (@SummrWrites), Twitter, February 28, 2019, 11:06 p.m.

autonomous as human individuals. We act like the members of the Trinity are in heaven playing card games as we go about murdering millions of his unborn image-bearers. The rejection of the Born-Alive Act by the United States Senate is nothing short of political Molechism, tantamount to the sacrificing of children to the heathen god, Molech, in the Old Testament (Leviticus 18:21).

The defeat of the Born-Alive Act is evidence that men and women who are of depraved minds are serving in Congress today. Sadly, many of these politicians are there because people who profess to be Christian voted for them. And in that sense, the blood of countless children who are born alive but will die because of this legislation not passing is on our hands. May our ever-merciful God have mercy on us.

Discussion Questions

1. Democrats and Republicans could not come together to pass the Born-Alive Act. Why is this significant to remember? Why do we say that abortion is a theological issue rather than a political one?
2. According to the chapter, what is the role Christians play in advocating a Christian worldview when going to the polls to vote?
3. What are the common arguments by those advocating for abortion, and how have these arguments impacted the church?
4. How would you argue an anti-abortion position from Scripture?
5. What role does theology play in your politics?

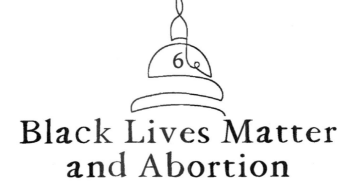

Black Lives Matter and Abortion

On July 6, 2019, the *New York Times* published an article written by John Eligon entitled "When 'Black Lives Matter' Is Invoked in the Abortion Debate." The article features an interview with three individuals, each of whom is black: Rev. Clint Stancil, pastor of Wayman A.M.E. Church in St. Louis, Missouri; Ms. Kawanna Shannon, director of surgical services at the Planned Parenthood clinic in St. Louis; and Rev. Michael Jones, pastor of Friendly Temple Missionary Baptist Church in St. Louis.

Now, if the title of the article itself didn't grab your attention, perhaps the very first paragraph will, as it is clear evidence of the ideological direction the article intends to take: "As a pastor, Clinton Stancil counsels his black congregants that abortion is akin to the taking of innocent life. But as a civil rights activist, Mr. Stancil urges them to understand the social forces that prompt black women to have abortions at disproportionately high rates."[1]

---

[1] John Eligon, "When 'Black Lives Matter' Is Invoked in the Abortion Debate," *The New York Times*, July 6, 2019, https://www.nytimes.com/2019/07/06/us/black-abortion-missouri.html.

Go back and read that once more. You undoubtedly registered all kinds of issues just with the opening statement of the article. At first glance, it appears that Rev. Stancil has nuanced his position to such a level that where Scripture has placed a period, he has placed a comma in an effort to move the bar. This type of nuance is simply an effort to cloud the issue and clear the way for sin.

Another thing that immediately stands out about this article is that the *New York Times* chose to interview three ideological and theological black progressives on this issue in an apparent and deliberate effort to push the narrative that the high abortion rate among black women is a matter of socioeconomic factors and influences. It is that same narrative that has been propagated for the last eighty years, going all the way back to the implementation of Margaret Sanger's "Negro Project" in 1939—which, ironically, was facilitated with the willing help of black pastors whom Sanger strategically engaged for the sole purpose of propagating that narrative to poor black families, especially in the South.

Consider what Margaret Sanger wrote in a December 1939 letter to Dr. Clarence James Gamble, then-president of the Pathfinder Fund, which provided financial backing and support to pro-abortion organizations. Like Sanger, Dr. Gamble was a eugenicist and an ardent supporter of abortion. An interesting nugget about Gamble is that he was also the grandson of James Gamble, co-founder of the Procter & Gamble Corporation, and heir to the Gamble family fortune. In the letter to Dr. Gamble, Margaret Sanger wrote:

> There is only one thing that I would like to be in touch with you about and that is the Negro Project of the South which, if the execution of the details remain in Miss Rose's hands, my suggestions will not be confusing because she knows the way my mind works. Miss Rose sent me a copy of your letter of December 5th and I note that you doubt it worthwhile to employ a full time Negro physician. It seems to me from my experience where I have been in North Carolina, Georgia, Tennessee and Texas, that while the colored Negroes have great respect for white doctors they can get closer to their own members and more or less lay their cards on the table which means their ignorance, superstitions

and doubts. They do not do this with the white people and if we can train the Negro doctor at the Clinic he can go among them with enthusiasm and with knowledge, which, I believe, will have far-reaching results among the colored people. His work in my opinion should be entirely with the Negro profession and the nurses, hospital, social workers, as well as the County's white doctors. His success will depend upon his personality and his training by us. The [black] ministers' work is also important and also he should be trained, perhaps by the Federation as to our ideals and the goal that we hope to reach. We do not want word to go out that we want to exterminate the Negro population and the minister is the man who can straighten out that idea if it ever occurs to any of their more rebellious members.[2]

Too Black and Too Poor

The narrative being advanced by the three individuals featured in this *New York Times* article—that high abortion rates among black women is a consequence of "social forces"—is not new. In fact, it's been around for a very long time. Our question, then, is this: if so-called social forces are the material cause of high abortion rates among black women, why aren't those same social forces the cause of the sexual intercourse these women engage in that result in their becoming pregnant in the first place? I mean, if you're too poor to have the baby, then why aren't you too poor to have the sexual intercourse that resulted in the baby?

Poverty, of course, is relative. Most people entering this country illegally have no issue with the "poverty" they find in America. Furthermore, what is the economic threshold required for someone to understand that unprotected sex results in a child? It's as if the bar of intelligence continues to move with each issue raised. The first issue is race, as if black people are too stupid to know that sex results in a baby. Then the economic issue is added, as if black people are too stupid and too poor to know that sex results in a baby. People have been having babies since the beginning of time; knowledge of this

---

2 Margaret Sanger, "Letter to Dr. C.J. Gamble," December 10, 1939, Genius, accessed June 16, 2021, https://genius.com/2808563.

truth doesn't require a specific dollar amount or a particular level of melanin in one's skin.

What these religious leaders are saying is that blacks are far too black and far too poor to realize that sexual intercourse results in having a baby. Therefore, we can't blame them for having a murderous heart that desires to kill their babies in the womb.

To espouse this position requires heavy reliance on nuance. But those leveraging nuance cloud it in colorful language so as to sound erudite and scholarly. It's high time that we call out these nuances for what they are. They are appeals built on the fact that these men and women think that black people are far too stupid to know what they are doing, and since they cannot control themselves, we cannot lay any blame to their charge.

White Legislators and Our Women

Moving beyond the first paragraph, the article goes on to say that

> the national debate over abortion has focused of late on when a heartbeat is discernible in the fetus, on the rights of women to make choices over their bodies and on the vast schism between the opposing views on ending pregnancies.
>
> But to many African-Americans like Mr. Stancil, who is the pastor of Wayman A.M.E. Church in St. Louis, abortion cannot be debated without considering the quality of urban schools. Or the disproportionately high unemployment rate in black communities. Or the significant racial disparities in health care.
>
> "As much as I believe with all my heart about the killing, the taking of innocent lives, I also believe that I will never support giving white legislators who have no interest in our community the ability to tell our women what they can do with their bodies," Mr. Stancil said of sweeping abortion restrictions recently approved in Missouri.[3]

First, Stancil is a bigot for what he said about "white legislators" and needs to repent of his sinful partiality. Second, does Stancil believe

---

3 Eligon, "When 'Black Lives Matter.'"

that only black legislators have "the ability to tell our women what they can do with their bodies?"

Don't miss the fact that Stancil referred to the black women who are having these abortions as "our women." That kind of language reeks of the kind of ethnic tribalism so prevalent among black Americans, compounded by this man's implication that white legislators, because they're white, have no say in protecting unborn black children! Stancil isn't a reverend; he's a racist!

It is interesting that Stancil uses language like "our women" to denote some sense of belonging to a group but never uses language like "our women" to denote the kind of responsibility a man should truly have for a woman. "Our women" are left as single mothers by 72 percent of men who leave them to raise babies on their own. Yet Stancil can't seem to address that issue. "Our women" are suffering the burden of raising most of those babies in poverty. Where is Stancil on that? "Our women" suffer the scars of depression from the murder of their own children in the womb. Again, Stancil is silent.

Instead, the argument Stancil raises is one that winks at sin as he parrots the morally evil arguments of the culture: "my body, my choice." The fact that he uses racism and division to silence "white legislators" advocating for black lives takes his wickedness to an even greater level of moral depravity. What difference is a legislator's ethnicity to an unborn child whose brains are being sucked out for profit at a Planned Parenthood clinic? These aren't the words of a true man of God but of the vilest kind of racist clothed in religious vestments.

The Hatred of the Woke

Stancil's argument is a prime example of the kind of tribalist idiocy that arises from embracing the "gospel" of social justice. Everything—even the most fundamental of orthodox biblical principles, in this case, that life begins at conception and that every life that is conceived is conceived bearing the image of God at the moment of conception (Genesis 1:27)—is filtered through the nuanced lens of ethnicity and what's most important to a particular ethnic "tribe."

Considering the other aspects of Stancil's comments gives rise to another question we would love to ask the reverend. What in the world does the quality of urban schools or the disproportionately high unemployment rate in black communities or the significant racial disparities in health care have to do with forcibly inserting a pair of forceps into the brain of an unborn child so that he or she dies an excruciatingly painful death because of "social forces"? How in the world are any of those things germane to the fundamental issue of murdering an unborn child in the womb? After all, we're talking about children who will never have an opportunity to go to school or apply for a job or have children themselves. What kind of woke thinking is this?

We are convinced that those who promote woke thinking possess an inherent hatred of the very people they claim to be helping. How else can you explain the position of Stancil, who as a reverend should know the ravages of sin on the human condition? Here's a guy who, rather than addressing the sin of murder, pulls a Genesis 3, "Did God really say?" as he moves the bar away from sin, pointing to other issues as the culprit. This is ludicrous.

Stancil should know better than most that these women will give an account to God for the murder of their child. On that final day they will not be able to say it was poor schools, unemployment, and racial disparities in health care that caused them to murder their children. God will not find these excuses particularly satisfying to the wrath that will be due for their actions. As a reverend, Stancil, of all people, knows this. Stancil himself must repent. As one who operates in the office of a teacher, his judgment will be even stricter. He, too, is complicit in the murder of all the babies whose mothers listened to his advice and followed through with murder.

This is exactly what we mean by saying that those who promote woke thinking possess an inherent hatred of the very people they claim to be helping. Apart from repentance of the sin of murder in abortion and the saving knowledge of Jesus Christ, these women will find themselves rightly deserving the wrath of God. How much must you hate a person to encourage them in their path toward eternal judgment?

Circumstances and Partiality

Here's more from the *New York Times* article:

> In many black communities, the abortion debate is inextricably tied to race in ways that white communities seldom confront. Social and economic disparities that are particularly challenging to African-Americans, from mass incarceration to maternal and infant mortality, are crucial parts of that discussion.
>
> The best way to reduce abortions, many black people both for and against the practice argue, is to address the difficult circumstances that lead so many black women to end their pregnancies.[4]

Read that final sentence again. What are the "difficult circumstances that lead so many black women to end their pregnancies"? Are those the same "difficult circumstances" that existed before they got pregnant? Or did those circumstances just magically appear after they realized they were pregnant? Why isn't the solution to abortion to abstain from premarital sexual intercourse, which is the only certain way to not become pregnant?

Additionally, how are white people obligated to concern themselves with the "social and economic disparities that are particularly challenging to African-Americans" when those economic disparities had no bearing whatsoever on the volitional decision a woman makes to engage in sexual intercourse at the risk of becoming pregnant? How are white people responsible for that? Social disparities never got anyone pregnant.

In the area of abortion, Stancil and others like him give black women a pass on murder because of "difficult circumstances." Contrast this idea with what Scripture says about the sin of partiality:

- "I solemnly charge you in the presence of God and of Christ Jesus and of His chosen angels, to maintain these principles without bias, doing nothing in a spirit of partiality" (1 Timothy 5:21).

---

4 Eligon, "When 'Black Lives Matter.'"

- "You shall not show partiality in judgment; you shall hear the small and the great alike" (Deuteronomy 1:17).
- "To show partiality is not good, because for a piece of bread a man will transgress" (Proverbs 28:21).
- "You shall do no injustice in judgment; you shall not be partial to the poor nor defer to the great, but you are to judge your neighbor fairly" (Leviticus 19:15).

When held up against the commands of God, Mr. Stancil and those who agree with him are shown to be guilty of the sin of ethnic partiality and must repent. The office of pastor and the ecclesiastical title of reverend have not prevented Stancil's ethnic prejudice toward white people, which causes him to see even the murder of unborn children through race-colored glasses. Men such as this are not demonstrating that they have a saving knowledge of Jesus Christ, and certainly shouldn't be in a pulpit!

Of course, it is not merely religious leaders like Stancil who espouse partiality in matters of sexual sin. The problem is far more pernicious. In our current culture we often treat sex like air. We've elevated sexual activity to the position that it's a requirement for life, just like breathing, so we can justify whatever deviant sexual proclivity or consequence from sexual activity that follows. Avoiding sexual activity, therefore, is simply impossible. Since premarital sexual activity is immutable (i.e., unchangeable—an attribute that should only be attributed to God), we've decided that everything else in culture must be moved to suit the "god of my own sexuality."

We see this in every area of life, from debates about gender fluidity to homosexuality to even pederasty and pedophilia. The mantras in these arguments are all the same: they can't help how they were born, or in this instance, they can't be charged with sin since they didn't have the social-economic structures in place to keep this from happening. The message is, it is not their fault; instead, it's someone else's fault—someone with power structures and money. It's ridiculous.

Responsibility or Reparations?

Continuing through the *New York Times* article, we read,

> Underlying the debate is the rich heritage of the black church, at once a liberal center of civil rights activism and an institution that preaches religious conservatism. In discussions with African-American congregants, the abortion debate can often feel like wading through a series of contradictions. Mr. Stancil, for instance, opposes abortions but is also against far-reaching restrictions that would eliminate all access to them. Most black voters support legal access to abortion but are also split on whether abortion is morally acceptable.[5]

Now, we have to take issue with the article's description of the black church as "an institution that preaches religious conservatism." That might have been the reality at one time, but not anymore, at least not with regard to the black church as a whole. There may today be individual churches with predominantly black congregations that can be described as preaching religious conservatism, but from what we see today across the broader landscape of black ecclesiology, the "black church" is a liberal institution that sees itself primarily as a center of civil and social activism, as opposed to a center of gospel proclamation and evangelization in terms of calling people to repentance of sin and faith in Christ.

We say that in light of what is being preached in pulpits at predominantly black churches like Epiphany Fellowship Church in Philadelphia where Dr. Eric Mason, author of *Woke Church*, is lead pastor. Interestingly, it was that same Eric Mason who, in his book *Manhood Restored: How the Gospel Makes Men Whole*, says this: "We need fathers, and we're only going to be fathers to our children when we see that true fatherhood is rooted and defined in God the Father."[6] Where is that message in the "black church" today? We don't see it. Instead, we see more calls for making reparations to black families than for *repairing* black families.

---

5 Eligon, "When 'Black Lives Matter.'"
6 Eric Mason, *Manhood Restored: How the Gospel Makes Men Whole* (Nashville: Broadman & Holman, 2013), 3.

One reason for this is that repairing the family requires responsibility, and there are no calls for fathers to step up and be responsible. Repairing the family requires responsibility on the part of fathers who have acted in morally reprehensible ways by abandoning a woman they chose to have sex with. But there was no mention of fathers in the entire *New York Times* article. Neither is there mention of sex-charged hip-hop culture, where women are sexual objects to be used by men and discarded whenever necessary. Those weren't stated as part of the problem. Instead, we reach to "whites," social economics, and a lack of education as contributories to abortion.

Rather than personal responsibility, what seems to be preferred by our woke thought leaders today is repentance reparations. A perfect example is what Beto O'Rourke tried to do recently when he discovered that his ancestors held slaves. His response was that someone else (the taxpayers) should pay money since he benefited from this sin.

Sowing and Reaping

If the black church truly preached religious conservatism, this *New York Times* article would never have been written to begin with. Instead, the article says Mr. Stancil "opposes abortions but is also against far-reaching restrictions that would eliminate all access to them." What is "far-reaching" about wanting to keep the unborn image-bearers of God from being murdered in the womb? When is the church going to get back to preaching to our young people that there are consequences for your actions and that when you make decisions like this, you will reap what you sow?

God's Word states this unequivocally in Galatians 6:7: "Do not be deceived, God is not mocked; for whatever a man sows, this he will also reap." The church has got to get this message through to our young people that when you make the choice to violate God's precepts and commands, there will always be consequences, and God expects you to face those consequences biblically.

Psalm 15:1–4 is instructive: "O LORD, who may abide in Your tent? Who may dwell on Your holy hill? He who walks with integrity, and works righteousness, and speaks truth in his heart. He does not slander with his tongue, nor does evil to his neighbor, nor takes up a reproach against his friend; in whose eyes a reprobate is despised, but who honors those who fear the LORD; he swears *to his own hurt and does not change*" (emphasis added).

What the psalmist is saying is that God expects his people to be people of integrity, to respond rightly and righteously in any and all situations, regardless of how difficult it appears to be. This certainly holds true in those adverse situations that we've brought on ourselves because of our willful disobedience. In the case of conceiving a child through sexual immorality, it means confessing and repenting of your sin, accepting God's merciful forgiveness, and moving forward with your pregnancy, trusting that God will provide everything you need to make it through that situation.

Consider the example of the Israelites, who, upon realizing their sin in demanding a king, repented. Look at how the prophet Samuel responds:

> Then all the people said to Samuel, "Pray for your servants to the LORD your God, so that we may not die, for we have added to all our sins this evil by asking for ourselves a king." Samuel said to the people, "Do not fear. You have committed all this evil, yet do not turn aside from following the LORD, but serve the LORD with all your heart. You must not turn aside, for then you would go after futile things which can not profit or deliver, because they are futile." (1 Samuel 12:19–21)

Paul encouraged the church at Philippi to go to God with their needs: "Be anxious for nothing, but in everything by prayer and supplication with thanksgiving let your requests be made known to God. . . . And my God will supply all your needs according to His riches in glory in Christ Jesus" (Philippians 4:6, 19).

Serving the God of Self

The biological facts are clear: whenever you have sexual intercourse, if you are a woman, there is a possibility you will become pregnant. That is a universal truth irrespective of what "social forces" might exist. The biological formula for conceiving a child is no different for poor women than for wealthy women. It is no different for black women than it is for white women, Hispanic women, Asian women, or any other ethnic group of women—and that principle applies across the board.

Rather than looking to the God who can "supply all [their] needs according to His riches in glory in Christ Jesus," women who have an abortion have decided that the god they serve is far too weak to see them through their situation. Sadly, they've been preached to by men (or women) who proffer an impotent, emotionally driven deity who recognizes his inability to care for needs and therefore "understands" if they end their baby's life. Accordingly, these women turn aside and go after the futile thing they think will fulfill their needs.

These women are not stupid, slow, or ignorant of what they are doing. We run into them at the abortion clinic regularly. Not one of them has acted as if they are unaware of what they are doing. In fact, they often brag about it. Many times, after we've offered them everything Stancil claims forces them to have an abortion, these women proudly enter the abortion clinic anyway, content to sacrifice their child on the altar of convenience as they serve the god of self.

Ms. Kawanna Shannon, of the Planned Parenthood clinic in St. Louis, clearly articulated this perspective in her interview with the *New York Times*:

> "About half the women who received abortions at the clinic last year were black. The clinic also provides other health care services, and supporters worry that patients from marginalized communities will face the biggest consequences if abortion access in the state is eliminated, including turning to risky, illegal means to terminate pregnancies. Black women already have enough challenges," said Kawanna Shannon, who is black and the director of surgical services at the clinic. "And now I have to still deal with the state and the governor now passing laws and telling me what I can and can't do with my own body," she said. "It's just burdensome."[7]

---

7 Eligon, "When 'Black Lives Matter.'"

In addition to appealing to the challenges faced by black women and arguing that illegal abortions would add to that burden, Ms. Shannon describes them as "patients from marginalized communities." How are these women being marginalized from having sexual intercourse to begin with? Why is it that these women are viewed as marginalized only *after* they've become pregnant?

The question bears repeating: if you're too poor to have the baby, why aren't you too poor to have the sexual intercourse that caused the baby? Furthermore, how did being from a marginalized community become code for being morally bankrupt? What's worse is that the opportunity to correct, instruct, rebuke, or reprove is removed since the lack of moral dignity is not the fault of the person committing the act of sin but some nebulous "community" with a myriad of issues for which no one has a solution.

Woke Theology

The article goes on to say,

> Religious teachings may have convinced some African-Americans that life begins in the womb. But having seen firsthand how their communities have been hurt by high incarceration rates, economic disinvestment and a lack of educational opportunities, some have a hard time embracing what they see as one-size-fits-all abortion bans. Dr. Bobo, a minister from Kansas City, said he counsels women not to have abortions, but at the end of the day, "It's her choice. I cannot manipulate her into agreeing; I cannot guilt her," he said. Mr. Stancil of the Wayman A.M.E. Church said his view that abortion amounted to ending a life was compatible with his belief in a woman's choice because God was the ultimate judge.[8]

The excuses of black communities hurt by "high incarceration rates, economic disinvestment and a lack of education opportunities" is shaky at best. We've never talked to anyone who has been incarcerated for being black, although maybe that was true in this country in the past. However, in the days of 72-percent single motherhood in the black communities, we have not known anyone who was a victim of

---
8 Eligon, "When 'Black Lives Matter.'"

being imprisoned for being black. As for economic divestment, the color of money is green. We are aware of things like Black Wall Street, especially as Virgil is from Tulsa, Oklahoma. But that happened in 1921, and it wasn't until 1965 that the black single mother birth rate rose to 25 percent. We would argue that things were much more difficult for blacks in 1965 than they are in 2021. As for the "lack of educational opportunities," in an era of colleges advocating affirmative action for decades and the age where everyone who has a smartphone has access to the world of knowledge and information, blacks have more opportunities to avoid ignorance than ever before. All this is a ruse to murder black babies and allow these false teachers the opportunity to cover themselves in the temporary warmth of a cold lie.

Incarceration rates, economic divestment, and lack of educational opportunities have nothing to do with murdering an unborn child. What Mr. Stancil and Dr. Bobo are preaching is pure, unadulterated "woke theology." Stancil particularly is so culturally aware that the theology he is preaching is neck deep in nuance. In an attempt to excuse himself for tossing aside the biblical truth that every human being who is conceived bears the image of God and for that reason alone deserves to not have its life snuffed out at an abortion clinic, he appeals to God as the ultimate judge.

The Whole Gospel

Yet there are no asterisks in the Word of God. Yes, ultimately, as with every opportunity to obey God or not, the individual must make the decision. But to proffer the notion that subjectively viewed social injustices are valid reasons for ending a life that has been created by virtue of a willful choice is both ridiculous and inexcusable. In his providence, God has so ordered this world that we reap consequences for our actions, and he calls us to act responsibly when we encounter those consequences.

If you willfully refuse to make the monthly payments for the house on which you took out a mortgage, you should expect your home to be foreclosed on and you and your family evicted from that residence. You understand that when you read through the mortgage disclosure documents. The same principle applies to pregnancy and abortion.

"Social forces" have nothing to do with your volitional decision to have sexual intercourse and risk getting pregnant. And when and if you do get pregnant, it is not that unborn child who should pay the price for the sinful choice you made.

This argument holds true even in the case of pregnancy resulting from rape. Even in the sin of rape, the unborn child is a human being created in the image of God. How in the world does the murder of this unique individual adjudicate the wicked evil inflicted upon a woman by the father? It doesn't. It only adds to the woman's charge and conscience the bloodguilt of the murder of her child.

It's long past time for the church, and black churches especially, to stop using social injustice as an excuse for not preaching the whole counsel of God. Young black men and women need to hear the gospel—the *whole* gospel—which includes that sexual intercourse outside of marriage is a sin, and that murdering an unborn child is a sin regardless of what "social forces" may exist.

There was a time when black churches preached this to their congregations. They preached unashamedly and with authority what God regarded as sin. It's one reason why abortion rates and divorce rates in black communities were so low prior to the 1960s, before the decimating effects of the welfare state, with its mirage of a better life, became a reality.

The *New York Times* article continues: "The Rev. Michael Jones, the pastor at Friendly Temple Missionary Baptist Church in St. Louis, said that he believed in preserving life, but that he did not 'have the power to take away that choice' a woman makes on an abortion. Regardless of what happens with the Planned Parenthood clinic in St. Louis, Mr. Jones said his focus was on the church's efforts to help and empower black lives."[9] And there you have it. That's how Black Lives Matter is invoked in the abortion debate—by redefining the mission of the church from proclaiming the gospel of salvation in Jesus Christ to helping and empowering black lives only.

That's a "woke church" right there.

---

9 Eligon, "When 'Black Lives Matter.'"

Discussion Questions

1. What was the Negro Project, and what role did Margaret Sanger play in implementing it?
2. What are "social forces," and what is the role they play in high abortion rates in the black community?
3. What role does poverty play in high abortion rates, and how does modern-day poverty impact those numbers?
4. According to the chapter, how has the social justice gospel impacted abortion rates?
5. What was the rate of single motherhood in the black community in 1965? Compare that to the single motherhood rate in the black community today. What has changed?

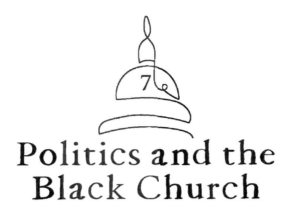

Politics and the Black Church

On November 2, 2019, Bishop Paul S. Morton, founder of the Full Gospel Baptist Church Fellowship International (FGBCFI), sent the following tweet from his personal Twitter account referencing then-presidential candidate Pete Buttigieg: "Dems [Democrats] I pray U will use wisdom in voting. Being too liberal will not win. I am not Homophobic. But it is definitely not the time 4 POTUS 2b a man with his husband up there by his side. There are those of us who love everybody But we believe in the Biblical Definition of Marriage."[1]

The following are just a sample of some of the comments Morton received in response to the tweet:

"Wow this is homophobic."[2]

"This is ugly, terrible, misguided and mean."[3]

"And this is why people are leaving the church."[4]

---
1 Bishop Paul S Morton (@BishopPMorton), Twitter, November 2, 2019, 8:01 a.m.
2 Harrison (@HarrisonPrak), Twitter, November 2, 2019, 6:24 p.m.
3 Andrea Morgan (@AndreaDMorgan), Twitter, November 2, 2019, 6:26 p.m.
4 EES (@IIEESEEII), Twitter, November 2, 2019, 10:44 p.m.

"This is literally the reason I left the church. There is no need for this hatred from you or from any pulpit. You're an absolute embarrassment."[5]

"Go 2 Hell."[6]

"That's homophobia. Stop using the bible to defend your bigotry."[7]

"People who say they're not homophobic are the ones who most definitely are. This is ridiculous and shameful."[8]

"Hate is a sad legacy for a book that tells us the greatest commandment is to LOVE God with all our heart, soul, and mind, and to LOVE our neighbors as ourselves."[9]

"You are not a Christian, not with this hate in your heart."[10]

Bishop Morton's name only draws this much attention one or twice every four years when he, like his contemporaries, can be counted on to deliver the black masses to vote for a particular Democratic candidate. But when Morton speaks, he is not simply representing himself in his comments. In 2020, the FGBCFI claimed more than eight hundred affiliated churches across the United States.[11] As the founding bishop, he has an important voice in the black circles he represents.

Theology and Politics

Our reason for highlighting Bishop Morton's tweet has less to do with his politics or who he suggests Christians support for president in 2020 and more to do with how the theology of professing Christians influences whom they support for political office. Morton's tweet,

---

5 Joshua Grotheer (@joshuagrotheer), Twitter, November 2, 2019, 8:30 p.m.
6 Brian Box Brown (@boxbrown), Twitter, November 2, 2019, 6:27 p.m.
7 LJ (@ljohn44)., Twitter, November 2, 2019, 6:24 p.m..
8 Missy Votes Blue! (@KCAZgirl), Twitter, November 2, 2019, 5:47 p.m.
9 Vaughn Judge Jr. (@SixFootLive), Twitter, November 3, 2019, 8:48 p.m.
10 mary is unrelentlessly upset (@stringoflightsx), Twitter, November 2, 2019, 6:28 p.m.
11 "Locations – Full Gospel Baptist," accessed May 20, 2021, https://www.fullgospelbaptist.org/locations.

and the subsequent responses to it, raise a much larger and more significant question than what political candidate to support: As Christians, to what degree *does* or *should* our theological worldview shape our political worldview?

That question intrinsically presupposes that those who profess to be Christian are truly regenerate in accordance with John 1:12–13 and, assuming the first to be true, that the theology to which those regenerate believers subscribe is biblically orthodox. This is critical, as theologian Wayne Grudem says in his book *Politics According to the Bible*. Grudem argues that as Christians consider where we stand on certain political issues, we must frame our positions in light of such foundational questions as these: What does the Bible say about (1) God as creator, (2) the world he created, (3) us as human beings created in his image, (4) sin, and (5) God's purpose for putting human beings on the earth in the first place?[12]

It is in light of those kinds of theological questions that Bishop Paul Morton exhorts Christians to seriously consider the biblical implications of aligning politically with a biological male who is "married" to another biological male. While there are significant theological areas where we disagree with Morton, in this tweet, he gets it right. Morton isn't merely suggesting that Christians not support Pete Buttigieg because Morton disagrees with Buttigieg's positions on issues such as taxes, the economy, or foreign policy. These are all issues about which people can and are expected to have varying opinions. Morton, however, appeals in his tweet to the authority of God's Word and what his Word teaches about marriage.

Black or Godly?

To place this in a somewhat broader context, it should be noted that in the presidential elections held in 2008 and 2012, millions of professing evangelical Christians voted for Barack Obama, and no voting bloc supported Obama in greater numbers during those two election cycles than did black evangelical Christians. They did that even

---

12 Wayne Grudem, *Politics According to the Bible: A Comprehensive Resource for Understanding Modern Political Issues in Light of Scripture* (Grand Rapids: Zondervan, 2010), 18.

though Obama openly and blatantly advocated and promoted a view of marriage that was egregiously unbiblical. In fact, in an interview with Robin Roberts of ABC News on May 9, 2012, then-president Barack Obama said, "I've just concluded that for me personally it is important for me to go ahead and affirm that I think same-sex couples should be able to get married."[13]

It's interesting to note the hypocrisy demonstrated by Bishop Morton. Why the change of heart on the issue in 2019? President Obama felt the same about the issue of so-called same-sex marriage, but Morton did not offer any challenge to the idea of voting for Obama on that basis. In fact, Bishop Morton provided no standard for allowing one's faith to inform their decision to vote at all when he delivered his congregations overwhelmingly to Obama during his presidential runs. But after the original dustup from Morton's Buttigieg tweet, the bishop began using Obama as cover concerning his current position:

> In 2008 LGBT was hard on P. Obama b/c he held fast he believed the biblical definition of marriage. We voted 4 him overwhelmingly. Never was called homophobic At end of 1st term he evolved 2 believe SSM. But the bible has not changed. Me either. So I'm not homophobic I'm Biblical[14]

> I love Pres Obama but b/c he changed & caused many of U 2 change that did not mean I had 2. The bible has not changed I Still Believe The Bible. In the Bible God allows U2 Choose. Ur Choice is Ur Choice My Choice is My Choice & I hv right 2 tweet who I think can win & who can't[15]

What appears to be happening is a systematic approach to theology informed by the whims of a particular candidate as long as they are a Democrat and especially if they are black. That's a problem.

---

13 Mackenzie Weinger, "Evolve: Obama gay marriage quotes," POLITICO, May 9, 2012, https://www.politico.com/story/2012/05/evolve-obama-gay-marriage-quotes-076109.
14 Bishop Paul S Morton (@BishopPMorton), Twitter, November 3, 2019, 9:00 a.m.
15 Bishop Paul S Morton (@BishopPMorton), Twitter, November 3, 2019, 9:30 a.m.

Now the tweet Paul Morton sent was not addressed to or targeted at any specific ethnic group, but one can safely deduce, especially given that the two churches Morton pastors are overwhelmingly black in terms of the ethnic composition of its congregations, that it is primarily, though perhaps not exclusively, to voters who identify as black and Christian that he is speaking. That Morton would have that particular demographic in mind is perfectly understandable given that 95 percent of black Americans voted for Obama in 2008 and around that same percentage in 2012, despite the fact that he supported homosexual marriage.[16]

When it comes to black professing Christians and politics, it's interesting that the issue of homosexual marriage seems to be the one issue that consistently serves as the primary litmus test in determining just how far left black Christians—a group that historically has been perceived to be theologically conservative yet politically liberal—are willing to go in expressing their support for a particular political candidate.

For example, on May 17, 2012, *The Christian Post* ran an article in which it quoted Bishop Harry Jackson Jr., senior pastor at Hope Christian Church in Baltimore, Maryland, as saying that many black Christians were in an "adulterous relationship" with then-President Barack Obama over the issue of homosexual marriage. In the article, Bishop Jackson is quoted as saying, "Obama laid down the gauntlet on black leaders. The question we are being forced to address is 'are you going to be black or be godly.'"[17]

Sadly, the black church has been indoctrinated with critical race theory and black liberation theology for so long, its hermeneutics have

---

16 Claire Cohen, "Breakdown of demographics reveals how black voters swept Obama into White House," *Daily Mail Online*, November 5, 2008, https://www.dailymail.co.uk/news/article-1083335/Breakdown-demographics-reveals-black-voters-swept-Obama-White-House.html; Peter Grier, "Election Results 2012: Who Won It for Obama?" *The Christian Science Monitor*, November 7, 2012, https://www.csmonitor.com/USA/Politics/Decoder/2012/1107/Election-results-2012-Who-won-it-for-Obama.
17 Paul Stanley, "Black Christians in an 'Adulterous' Relationship With Obama, Says Evangelical Pastor" *The Christian Post*, May 17, 2012, https://www.christianpost.com/news/black-christians-in-an-adulterous-relationship-with-obama-says-evangelical-pastor.html.

been corrupted by the broken lens of sinful racism. We've abandoned sound doctrine for sensational emotionalism, which speaks to the ever-moving target of the hearts of black folks. Of course, we know what Scripture says about trusting our corrupt human hearts: "The heart is more deceitful than all else and is desperately sick; who can understand it?"(Jeremiah 17:9).

The question that Bishop Paul S. Morton asked black Democrat Christian voters in his tweet was "Are you going to be a Democrat or be godly?" And, frankly, that's a question every Christian, not just black Christians, need to answer, regardless of political party allegiance or ideological persuasion.

Which Comes First?

It's essentially the question of which came first: the chicken or the egg? When we as Christians step into the voting booth to cast our vote for a particular candidate, which comes first: our political identity as a Democrat or Republican or our spiritual identity as followers of Jesus Christ?

Consider the words of A. W. Tozer in his book *Culture: Living as Citizens of Heaven on Earth*:

> The Christian faith, based upon the New Testament, teaches the complete antithesis between the Church and the world. It is no more than a religious platitude to say that the trouble with us today is that we have tried to bridge the gulf between two opposites, the world and the Church, and have performed an illicit marriage for which there is no biblical authority. Actually, no real union between the world and the Church is possible. When the Church joins up with the world, it is the true Church no longer, but only a pitiful hybrid thing, an object of smiling contempt to the world and an abomination to the Lord. The twilight in which many (or should I say most?) believers walk today is not caused by any vagueness on the part of the Bible. Nothing could be clearer than the pronouncements of the Scriptures on the Christian's relation to the world. The confusion that gathers around this matter results from the unwillingness of professing Christians to take the

Word of the Lord seriously. Christianity is so entangled with the world that millions never guess how radically they have missed the New Testament pattern. Compromise is everywhere. The world is whitewashed just enough to pass inspection by blind men posing as believers, and those same believers are everlastingly seeking to gain acceptance by the world. By mutual concessions men who call themselves Christians manage to get on with men who have for the things of God nothing but quiet contempt.[18]

Regardless of the issue of ethnicity, we all face the temptation to place political identity above informed theology. But as Christians we have an obligation to think clearly about these issues. Politics is theological. Our political policymaking should be informed by the theological foundations evident from a Christian worldview. The sad truth is that far too few Christians have any idea there is a way to view the world from a biblical framework. But Scripture is clear that the goal for believers is to be equipped in such a way so as not to be tossed by every wave of doctrine:

> He gave some as apostles, and some as prophets, and some as evangelists, and some as pastors and teachers, for the equipping of the saints for the work of service, to the building up of the body of Christ; until we all attain to the unity of the faith, and of the knowledge of the Son of God, to a mature man, to the measure of the stature which belongs to the fullness of Christ. As a result, we are no longer to be children, tossed here and there by waves and carried about by every wind of doctrine, by the trickery of men, by craftiness in deceitful scheming. (Ephesians 4:11–14)

We seem to want to buy into the notion of doctrine as something that only takes place inside the walls of a church between the hours of 8:00 a.m. and 12:00 p.m. on Sunday mornings. After the service is over, we no longer want to remain biblically informed for the purpose of living lives that honor God in all times, places, and seasons as he would have us do.

---

18 A. W. Tozer, *Culture: Living as Citizens of Heaven on Earth: Collected Insights from A. W. Tozer* (Chicago: Moody, 2016), 123–124.

Compartmentalized Theology

That so many people would be upset at Bishop Paul Morton's urging black Christians to stand on what the Word of God says about marriage says a lot about the spiritual state of the evangelical church in America in general and in the "black church" in particular. The responses Morton received to his tweet were a case in point that many professing Christians do not hold to a biblical worldview. Their theology is compartmentalized in such a way that the Word of God is authoritative and applicable only to certain aspects of their life in this world.

The truth is that a dichotomy has existed for quite some time that is entirely unique when contrasted with other ethnic groups within evangelicalism. The dichotomy is that black Christians, motivated by a desire to do what benefits the collective as opposed to what benefits the individual, tend to segregate their theological convictions from their political convictions when it comes to whom they will support for political office.

Such was the case with Barack Obama.

One key reason why Obama was elected in 2008 and subsequently reelected in 2012 is because black evangelical Christians were able to compartmentalize their theological convictions from their political convictions. Hence, being motivated to a large extent by the opportunity to make political history by electing a dark-skinned person as president of the United States, they had no qualms about voting for someone who supported such unbiblical positions as abortion on demand and same-sex marriage. In other words, solely for the sake of making history in most cases, they willingly and volitionally set aside and subjugated the clear teachings of Scripture in favor of satiating their own personal desire to see someone elected president whose level of melanin was like theirs. But when you talk about making history, it is important to stop to consider what *kind* of history you're making.

Such tribalism, whether it be rooted in ethnicity, gender, culture, or political ideology, is no legitimate reason to vote for any person for political office. So where does that kind of attitude, particularly among black Christians, come from? What is the genesis of a mindset that partitions theology and politics so as to be convinced it is more benevolent to vote on the basis of the interests of the collective above those of the individual and to do so regardless of the potential consequences to the collective in whose interests you supposedly are acting?

Approaching Politics with a Renewed Mind

Again, what we're really talking about here is worldview, the obligation that believers in Jesus Christ have to view the world and everything in it, including our politics, through the lens of the objective truth of the Word of God. We say that in light of what we read in Romans 12:2, "Do not be conformed to this world, but be transformed by the renewing of your mind, so that you may prove what the will of God is, that which is good and acceptable and perfect."

A biblical worldview of politics holds that the teachings of Scripture are the primary basis on which our decisions regarding whom we will and won't support for political office are to be formed and shaped, not our own personal opinions, biases, or predilections or the personalities or positions of the individuals we may or may not be inclined to support. In the case of Pete Buttigieg, what Bishop Paul Morton exhorted black evangelical Christians to do is precisely what we just read in Romans 12:2. In the context of the "good and acceptable and perfect" will of God, we must consider the ethos of biblical marriage clearly taught in Scripture against the worldly ethos of marriage that Buttigieg, and millions of others, adhere and subscribe to.

When we think about how Romans 12:2 and the principle of the "renewed mind" should influence how believers in Christ approach the sphere of politics, we're reminded of what theologian Herman Bavinck wrote in his book *Christian Worldview*:

> Neither is religion a romantic mood, an aesthetic affection of the heart, a means to the adornment of our human nature, as though God were there for our sake and we were not here for his sake. But religion is more. It is something different from and higher than all

these things together. It is to serve God with all your mind, with all your soul, and with all your might, to make oneself a living, holy sacrifice pleasing to God; it is to trust unconditionally in God as the rock of our salvation and of our portion in eternity. The truth is objective; it exists independently of us. It does not direct itself toward us; we have to direct ourselves toward it. But just as the wisdom of God became flesh in Christ, so should the truth also enter us. In the path of freedom, it must become our personal and spiritual property; through a living and true faith, it must become constitutive of our thinking and doing and then spread outside us until the earth is full of the knowledge of the Lord.[19]

Bavinck is saying that the truth of the Word of God should guide believers in every aspect and avenue of our existence in this world. Or, to put it differently, those who profess to be Christians should strive to apply a biblical worldview to the issues and matters that encompass our life in this temporal world. That is what Bavinck means when he says the truth of God's Word must become "constitutive of our thinking *and* doing." Bavinck's thoughts are similar to what John Calvin said in his *Institutes of the Christian Religion*: "Every Christian, to be sure, should so train himself as to think that, as long as he lives, it is with God that he must deal. Knowing this, he will be ready to account to God for all his actions; his purposes will comply with God's will and be rooted in it."[20]

More than Homosexuality

We need to seriously consider what Bishop Paul Morton said in light of those words from John Calvin and Herman Bavinck. As we mentioned before, doctrinally, we disagree with Bishop Morton on many things. For example, he is a Full Gospel, Pentecostal continuationist, whereas we are Reformed cessationists who subscribe to the doctrines of grace. There couldn't possibly be more opposite ends of the theological spectrum. But on this matter of black Christian voters, and Christian voters in general, standing on the biblical definition of marriage, we believe he is absolutely correct.

---

19 Herman Bavinck, *Christian Worldview*, trans. Nathaniel Gray Sutanto, James Eglinton, and Cory C. Brock (Wheaton, IL: Crossway, 2019), 132–133.
20 John Calvin, *Institutes of the Christian Religion*, 791.

But we're not going to let Bishop Morton off the hook so easily. It is interesting that Morton chose to point out Buttigieg's homosexual marriage as the primary reason why black Christians should withhold their support from his presidential bid, as opposed to calling attention to the fact that Buttigieg also is an ardent supporter of abortion. After all, abortion has decimated black families more than any other ethnic group in this country. According to the Centers for Disease Control, nearly 40 percent of all abortions involve the murder of black children.[21] Why didn't Morton mention that as a reason why black Christians shouldn't vote for Buttigieg? Or how about the 77 percent of children born to black single mothers?[22] Bishop Morton is trying to be selectively indignant about certain sins that black Christians should be mindful of and not others. That's called hypocrisy.

The great nineteenth-century preacher Charles Haddon Spurgeon, in a sermon entitled "The Candle," which he preached on April 24, 1881, said this: "I long for the day when the precepts of the Christian religion shall be the rule among all classes of men, in all transactions. I often hear it said, 'Do not bring religion into politics.' This is precisely where it ought to be brought, and set there in the face of all men as on a candlestick."[23] We need men like this today, willing to speak up on matters of culture and politics from a biblical worldview. But it takes courage, something that is seriously lacking in today's churches. We have men in the church who are cowering to secular movements that are infiltrating the church instead of just standing on the objective truth of the Word of God. They are subjecting the gospel to secular whims of the world.

---

21 Emily Ward, "CDC: 36% of Abortions Abort Black Babies," CNSNews, November 28, 2018, https://www.cnsnews.com/news/article/emily-ward/blacks-make-134-population-36-abortions.
22 Paul Bedard, "77% black births to single moms, 49% for Hispanic immigrants," *Washington Examiner*, May 5, 2017, https://www.washingtonexaminer.com/77-black-births-to-single-moms-49-for-hispanic-immigrants.
23 Charles H. Spurgeon, "1594. The Candle," Answers in Genesis, modified December 8, 2014, https://answersingenesis.org/education/spurgeon-sermons/1594-the-candle.

The Elephant in the Room

As a Democratic presidential candidate, Pete Buttigieg spent significant amounts of money in outreach efforts to black voters in the South, with a particular focus on Georgia and South Carolina. One specific promise Buttigieg made that undoubtedly found wide appeal among that particular demographic was his pledge to "fight systemic racism wherever we find it."[24]

Buttigieg's pledge was an admirable one. After all, who of us does not desire to live in a society that functions within a paradigm of objective truth and justice? No one wants to live in an unjust society. But, notwithstanding his promise to ferret out and rid this nation of systemic racism, we wonder, what did candidate Buttigieg intend to do about the intra-ethnic racism expressed on an almost daily basis by black people toward other black people?

Such racism is the proverbial "elephant in the room" no one wants to talk about when it comes to racism and discrimination in America. The worst prejudice we've ever experienced has been at the hands of other black people—people who look just like us—not some white person. No white person has ever referred to us as "coon" or "Uncle Tom" or "academic nigga," but there have been plenty of black people over the years who have done that.

The reality is that Buttigieg, just like every other politician who makes promises such as this, has no ability to do anything about racism. He is not God. He cannot change the racism in the heart of any individual. These are merely empty promises that far too many are mesmerized by.

When you consider that sinful ethnic prejudice is fundamentally a matter of changing hearts and not changing laws, you'll come to realize that there is truly little any politician can do to remedy that societal malady, whether he or she is the president of the United States or the local school board president. As John MacArthur said in

---

[24] Tucker Higgins, "Pete Buttigieg makes big South Carolina ad buy as campaign seeks elusive black support," CNBC, November 14, 2019, https://www.cnbc.com/2019/11/14/buttigieg-makes-south-carolina-ad-buy-as-campaign-seeks-black-support.html.

his book *Christ's Call to Reform the Church*, "Political and social justice efforts are, at best, short-term, external solutions for society's moral ills, and they do nothing to address the personal, internal, dominant matter of sinful hearts that hate God, and can be rescued from eternal death only by faith in the Lord Jesus Christ."[25]

Saviors Are Not Elected

When all is said and done, black Christian voters must ask themselves, "Would a mere promise to address systemic racism or pay off your student loan debt be worth compromising on the gospel?" Those who would do so reveal that they are looking for a politician as a savior. They need to stop looking. The job of Savior was already filled about two thousand years ago. There is no job opening. There will be no job opening. Saviors are not elected.

The issues here are much larger than political party affiliation or allegiance. It has to do with whether professing believers in Christ will govern themselves by an all-encompassing biblical worldview that applies to every aspect of their existence in this world, including politics, or by a worldview that is analogous to children playing hopscotch, where you skip over the politics box on the hopscotch grid because that's the one area of your life to which the principles and precepts of God's Word do not apply. If you compartmentalize your theology from your politics, you have a hopscotch theology.

So, when it comes to politics, what is a Christian to do? Consider these words of wisdom from the renowned Princeton and Westminster theologian J. Gresham Machen from his classic book, *Christianity & Liberalism*: "If the Word of God be heeded, the Christian battle will be fought both with love and with faithfulness. Party passions and personal animosities will be put away, but on the other hand, even angels from heaven will be rejected if they preach a gospel different from the blessed gospel of the Cross. Every man must decide upon which side he will stand. God grant that we may decide aright."[26]

---

25 John MacArthur, *Christ's Call to Reform the Church* (Chicago: Moody, 2018), 10.
26 J. Gresham Machen, *Christianity & Liberalism* (Glendale, CA: Bibliotech, 2019), 150.

For the regenerate Christian, that decision must be on the side of God's Word, even if it goes against your tribalist tradition. As black evangelical Christians robotically vote for one party every election, even when that party goes against God's Word, dogmatically promoting abortion, the LGBTQ lifestyle, and same-sex marriage, no apologetic will justify their actions.

Discussion Questions

1. Given his status as a church leader, should Bishop Morton have made the tweet? If so, why? If not, why not?
2. According to the chapter, what are the two issues for which the black church has remained consistent?
3. How did those two issues change during the presidency of Barack Obama?
4. What was required for black churches to embrace Barack Obama, and why is that important for understanding the current state of the black church?
5. What is the process believers should use when examining the issues of culture?

Reparations

Hendly, what was next to the youngest of her seven children, got sick and died. Aunt Sissy ain't sorrowed much. She went straight up to old Masser and shouted in his face, "Praise God! Praise God! My little child is gone to Jesus. That's one child of mine you ain't never gonna sell."[1]

Major Ellison bought me and carried me to Mississippi. I didn't want to go. They 'zamine you just like they do a horse. They look at your teeth and pull your eyelids back and look at your eyes and feel you just like you was a horse. . . . He said, "Do you want us to buy you?" I said, "No, I don't want you to buy me. I want to stay here." He said, "We'll be nice to you and give you plenty to eat." I said, "No you won't have much to eat. . . . I'd rather stay here because I get plenty of pot liquor and bread and buttermilk and I don't want to go. I got plenty." I didn't know that wasn't lots to eat. . . . I went on home and the next day the old white woman whipped me and I said to myself, "I wish that old man had bought me." I didn't know he had bought me anyhow.[2]

---

[1] Nancy Wiggins, quoted in Julius Lester, *To Be a Slave* (New York: Puffin Books, 1967), 42.
[2] Anonymous, quoted in Lester, 49–51.

> I remember once when we was gonna have a meeting down in the woods near the river. Well, they made me the look out boy and when the paddy rollers come down the lane past the church, you see they was expecting that the niggers gonna hold a meeting that night. Well sir, they tell me to step out from the woods and let 'em see me. Well I does and the paddy rollers that was on horseback come a chasing after me, just a galloping down the lane to beat the band. Well, I was ahead of ' em and when they got almost up with me I just ducked into the woods. 'Course the paddy rollers didn't stop so quick. They kept on round the bend and then there came a screaming and a crying that would make you think that all hell done bust loose. Them old paddy rollers done ripped right into an old great line of grape vine that the slaves had stretched acrossed the path. . . . After that, old paddy rollers got wise and used to tie they horses and come creeping on the woods on foot until they find where this meeting was going on. Then they would rush in and start whipping and beating the slaves unmerciful. All this was done to keep you from serving God and do you know some of those devils was mean and sinful enough to say, "If I catch you here serving God, I'll beat you. You ain't got no time to serve God. We bought you to serve us."[3]

The sobering words of these first-person accounts of slavery set the stage for our consideration of a biblical understanding of the reparations debate. We begin here because we have a deep appreciation for slavery and the human suffering it caused both in the past and where it is still alive and well in the world today. There is a stereotypical notion that social conservatives, as we are, have no such understanding of slavery and the suffering it causes. This is simply not true. We do, however, recognize that there is vast ignorance surrounding the issue of slavery, and we are determined to examine the issue and that of reparations with biblical and historical honesty.

Historical Background

For context to these important issues, consider the words of esteemed economist and scholar Thomas Sowell from his book *Discrimination and Disparities*:

---

3 West Turner, quoted in Lester, 104–105.

The confining of discussions of slavery to that of blacks held in bondage by whites is just one of the many ways in which the agendas of the present distort our understanding of the past, forfeiting valuable lessons that an unfiltered knowledge of the past could teach. At a minimum, the worldwide history of slavery should be a grim warning for all people, and for all time, against giving any human beings unbridled power over other human beings, regardless of how attractively that unbridled power might be packaged rhetorically. As Edmund Burke said, more than two centuries ago, "In history a great volume is unrolled for our instruction, drawing the materials of future wisdom from past errors and infirmities of mankind." But he warned that the past could also be a means of "keeping alive, or reviving, dissentions and animosities."[4]

To avoid the error of letting the agendas of the present distort our understanding of the past, we begin with a bit of personal background.

The Balanta

I, Darrell, am descended from an ethnic people known as the Balanta, the largest ethnic group in Guinea-Bissau, West Africa, representing more than one-quarter of the population and divided into four subgroups. An agricultural people, the Balanta primarily raise rice and practice spiritualism mixed with Islam or Catholicism. To the Balanta, God is believed to be far away.

This people, *my* people, were not victims of the transatlantic slave trade as goes the common myth about every black person of African descent. To the contrary, in his book *Planting Rice and Harvesting Slaves: Transformations Along the Guinea-Bissau Coast*, historian Walter Hawthorne points out that the Balanta people were willing participants.

> Balanta communities conducted raids on distant strangers for captives, many of whom they traded to area merchants who exported them to the Americas as slaves . . . To merchants, Balanta traded captives, for which they received valuable imports,

---

4 Thomas Sowell, *Discrimination and Disparities* (New York: Hachette Book Group, 2019), 221–222.

especially iron, deposits of which were lacking on the coast. Iron gave Balanta the ability to forge strong defensive weapons and to step up agricultural production. With iron-reinforced tools, Balanta adopted and developed sophisticated paddy rice farming techniques, producing surpluses of food that fed not shrinking, but growing populations. By planting rice and harvesting slaves, politically decentralized Balanta defended and provided for their communities. Slaves served this purpose as agricultural laborers, as wives or concubines, and as commodities that could be traded abroad for imported goods. The sale of some slaves brought income . . . and the retention of others brought labor for a host of endeavors.[5]

Before the Transatlantic Slave Trade

As we consider slavery reparations, we must first contextualize the issue by starting at the beginning—with slavery—not only in terms of its genesis in America with specific regard to black people (which dates to the early fifteenth century) but also many hundreds of years earlier in Africa. Case in point, the European transatlantic slave trade was preceded by many centuries by another, even more brutal, slave trade, one that in some parts of the world continues today. This is thoroughly documented in a book by Dr. Peter Hammond entitled *Slavery, Terrorism, and Islam: The Historical Roots and Contemporary Threat*, which adds to the context of the topic:

> While much has been written concerning the Trans-Atlantic slave trade, surprisingly little attention has been given to the Islamic slave trade across the Sahara, the Red Sea, and the Indian Ocean. While the European involvement in the Trans-Atlantic slave trade to the Americas lasted for just over three centuries, the Arab involvement in the slave trade has lasted fourteen centuries, and in some parts of the Muslim world is still continuing to this day. A comparison of the Islamic slave trade to the American slave trade reveals some interesting contrasts. While two out of every three slaves shipped across the Atlantic were men, the proportions were reversed in the Islamic slave

---

5 Walter Hawthorn, *Planting Rice and Harvesting Slaves: Transformations Along the Guinea-Bissau Coast* (Portsmouth, NJ: Heinemann, 2003), 1–2.

trade. Two women for every man were enslaved by the Muslims. While the mortality rate for slaves being transported across the Atlantic was as high as ten percent, the percentage of slaves dying in transit in the Trans-Sahara and East-African slave trade was between eighty and ninety percent. While almost all the slaves shipped across the Atlantic were for agricultural work, most of the slaves destined for the Muslim Middle East were for sexual exploitation as concubines in harems, and for military service.

While many children were born to slaves in the Americas, and millions of their descendants are citizens in Brazil and the United States to this day, very few descendants of the slaves that ended up in the Middle-East survived. While most slaves who went to the Americas could marry and have families, most of the male slaves destined for the Middle East slave bazaars were castrated, and most of the children born to the women were killed at birth. It is estimated that possibly as many as 11 million Africans were transported across the Atlantic (95 percent of which went to South and Central America, mainly to Portuguese, Spanish, and French possessions. Only 5 percent of the slaves went to the United States. However, at least 28 million Africans were enslaved in the Muslim Middle East. As at least 80 percent of those captured by Muslim slave traders were calculated to have died before reaching the slave markets, it is believed that the death toll from the 14 centuries of Muslim slave raids into Africa could have been over 112 million. When added to the number of those sold in the slave markets, the total number of African victims of the East-African slave trade could be as high as 140 million people.[6]

If we're going to have an intellectually honest conversation about reparations, it can happen only if we are willing to have an intellectually honest conversation about slavery, because slavery is why the vast majority of pro-reparationists are pro-reparations. To discuss the one and not the other, or, conversely, to discuss the latter *before* the former is to render the entire conversation moot and unnecessary.

---

6 Peter Hammond, *Slavery, Terrorism, and Islam: The Historical Roots and Contemporary Threat* (Manitou Springs, CO: Frontline Fellowship, USA, 2009), 12

Slavery in America

The truth is that there is a lot of ignorance out there about slavery, particularly as it relates to its origins in America. Much of what is being said about slavery in America, especially by those who argue in favor of paying reparations for slavery, is rooted in a faulty timeline about when slavery began in this nation and who was involved. For the most part, people's chronology of slavery in America starts with the 1860s and the Civil War era. Maybe one in ten people will accurately say it began in the 1600s when the first Africans arrived in Jamestown, Virginia. But for all the animosity and vitriol being aimed at white evangelicals today, and white people in general, for their role in slavery in America, the truth is black people not only played a significant role in facilitating the sale and transporting of slaves from Africa to America but also in owning them after they were here. Consider what author Larry Koger writes in his book *Black Slaveowners*:

> When the first federal census of 1790 was taken, the number of free colored slaveholders was quite small, but it gradually grew to a modest size. In 1790, the community of slaveholding colored persons stood at 59 slave masters who held 357 bondsmen. Within ten years, their numbers had declined to 45 slaveowners; however, the number of slaves held by the colored persons increased to 414. By 1820, the number of colored slaveholders began to grow significantly. The growth of the community of black slaveholders continued for the next 20 years. Between 1820 and 1830, the community of Afro-Americans who owned slaves increased by 95.6 percent. The rapid growth in the community of black slaveholders can be attributed to several factors. After 1820, free blacks who purchased kinsfolk or friends could not emancipate their loved ones without the approval of the state assembly, which seldom granted such manumissions. Consequently, the black slaveholders who normally would have freed their slaves were forced to hold their loved ones as chattel and report their kinsfolk as slaves to the census takers. Thus the normal process of decline through manumission was no longer a factor. Furthermore, the period from 1820 to 1840 witnessed the economic development of the free black community. Many

persons of color acquired the capital to purchase slaves. These new slaveowners were not related to their slaves by the bond of kinship; they bought these slaves to be used as laborers.[7]

Although the issue of black slave owners is almost never discussed, we must put the stereotypical myth that only white people owned slaves to rest once and for all. If we are going to deal openly and fairly with the topic of reparations, we must honestly account for everyone involved. The impact of slavery is widespread, beyond the United States and encompassing the whole world. Where this is recognized by pro-reparationists, there is a parallel tendency to maximize the horror of chattel slavery as something that has never been repeated anywhere on earth except in America. While we do not intend to minimize chattel slavery, we must point out that most reparation advocates seem to desire to play on the emotions of others, acting as if humanity has never before seen such levels of depravity until they had reached the shores of the United States. This myopic view of slavery leads to shortsighted solutions that would not hold up on a worldwide scale. Such solutions are a pointless exercise in futility.

Offering Expiation

With the broad scope of worldwide slavery as background, let's begin to look at the basics of the topic of reparations. We first need to answer these questions: What are *reparations*? What does that word mean? According to *Merriam-Webster*, the term *reparation* is defined as "the act of making amends, offering expiation, or giving satisfaction for a wrong or injury incurred."[8] We like that definition, especially "offering expiation," because expiation is a biblical concept.

In biblical terms, expiation has to do with taking away guilt through the payment of a penalty or the offering of an atonement: "When you were dead in your transgressions and the uncircumcision of your flesh, He made you alive together with Him, having forgiven us all our transgressions, having canceled out the certificate of debt consisting

---

7 Larry Koger, *Black Slaveowners* (Jefferson, NC: MacFarland & Company, 1985), 18–19.
8 *Merriam-Webster*, s.v., "reparation," accessed June 17, 2021, https://www.merriam-webster.com/dictionary/reparation.

of decrees against us, which was hostile to us; and He has taken it out of the way, having nailed it to the cross" (Colossians 2:13–14).

The phrase "canceled out" in this text is the Greek word *exaleiphō*, which translated means "to obliterate" or "to wipe out." It is a word that carries the idea of covering something with lime. So, when a person comes to faith in Christ, not only are their sins forgiven by God but he obliterates them, he wipes them out, he erases them, to never again be remembered against them. We see this same idea in Psalm 103:12, which reads, "As far as the east is from the west, so far has He removed our transgressions from us."

Now, the reason this idea of expiation is germane to our conversation about reparations is because many professing Christians today support paying reparations to black people since the atonement of Christ did not fully expiate or propitiate for the sins of past generations of believers who may have confessed and repented of the sin of slavery. Thus, they deem payment of reparations as the only way that such expiation or propitiation can be fully consummated. They won't acknowledge this, of course, but it's essentially the rationale on which their apologetic is based. In other words, it's not enough for these evangelical reparationists that Jesus Christ died on the cross to atone for sins like slavery. But now others—namely, white people—have to "atone" for those sins as well by paying reparations. These reparations are not to be given to people who were actual slaves but to people like the two of us, whose skin color happens to resemble people who were, in fact, slaves, although not all dark-skinned people are actually descended from slaves.

Remembering Sin

Such an attitude is heinously unbiblical, and we can see this by looking to the Scriptures. Let's look first at a couple of texts from the Old Testament:

- "Fathers shall not be put to death for their sons, nor shall sons be put to death for their fathers; everyone shall be put to death for his own sin" (Deuteronomy 24:16).

- "Yet you say, 'Why should the son not bear the punishment for the father's iniquity? When the son has practiced justice and righteousness and has observed all My statues and done them, he shall surely live. The person who sins will die. The son will not bear the punishment for the father's iniquity, nor will the father bear the punishment for the son's iniquity; the righteousness of the righteous will be upon himself, and the wickedness of the wicked will be upon himself. But if the wicked man turns from all his sins which he has committed and observes all My statutes and practices justice and righteousness, he shall surely live; he shall not die. All his transgressions which he has committed will not be remembered against him; because of his righteousness which he has practiced, he will live" (Ezekiel 18:19–22).

God says that for the person who repents of his sin, those sins "will not be remembered against him." But evangelical reparationists are in gross violation of this principle by doing exactly the opposite—they are "remembering" the past sins of others and holding those sins against their descendants! The word "remembered" in Ezekiel 18:22 is the Hebrew verb *zakar*, meaning "to call to mind" or "to make a memorial." This is *exactly* what evangelical reparationists are doing—they are making a "memorial" of the sin of slavery to obtain from the government and from non-government entities and institutions reparations for suffering they themselves never actually experienced.

To those individuals we pose these questions: Would you like God to treat your sin that way? How would it be for you to live each moment of every day being constantly reminded by a holy, righteous, and wrathful God of the sins you've committed against him? You could not endure such an existence for five seconds of your life! You would be as the psalmist who said in Psalm 130:3, "If You, LORD, should mark iniquities, O LORD, who could stand?" The answer, obviously, is no one. No one could stand before God were he to "remember" our sins against us—not even evangelical reparationists.

Vicarious Atonement, Individual Sin

Scripture is clear that the atonement of Christ on the cross is a *vicarious atonement*, which is to say, it is accomplished by Christ on behalf of others, namely, his elect. As 1 John 2:2 says, "He Himself is the propitiation [*hilasmos*, Greek for "appeasement" or "satisfaction"] for our sins; and not for ours only, but also for those of the whole world." But Scripture is also abundantly clear that the sins to which the vicarious atonement of Christ is applied are not vicarious. To suggest, as if by proxy, that a person must atone—whether in the form of reparations or some other material compensation—for sins that he or she did not actually commit is both unbiblical and absurd. No one sins vicariously, so why should anyone be recompensed vicariously for offenses never committed against them in actuality? In biblical terms, sin is very specific and attributable. In the same way, so is any restitution that might be warranted as recompense for those sins. We must also keep in mind that all sin is primarily and ultimately against God, which should relieve us from thinking we have any right to hold the sins of others against them.

When we talk about reparations for the sin of slavery in the United States, we are not talking about the sins of individuals living today. We are talking about the sins of their forefathers, and in the case of many, we don't even know if their ancestors participated in the sin of slavery. The assumption of guilt is based on the level of melanin in a person's skin. What racialists are demanding when they call for reparations, they demand of everyone with a certain melanin count rather than addressing personal sin in the life of the individual.

Our detractors will ask, "What about the temporal consequences of sin? Shouldn't sin have consequences?" Yes, sin does have consequences, so we respond, "Show us these individuals' sin, and it can be laid to their charge." But if we are going to reach back to what their forefathers did, we will find that is a dangerous road to walk. Can you imagine being brought up on charges today and being made to answer for the actions of your great-great-great-grandfather who did something sinful in the past? Even worldly justice doesn't work that way.

Specific and Attributable

What makes this whole notion of the government paying reparations for slavery to people who were never slaves so absurd is something we call *sin by proxy*. Sin by proxy is the unbiblical idea that the guilt of another person's presumed sin is somehow transferrable to someone else so that that person—by proxy—is now obligated to atone for someone's presumed sin by virtue of, in this case, paying reparations.

If we look into the Word of God, we will find universally objective principles that bear out that the idea of sin by proxy, particularly with regard to reparations, is unarguably an unbiblical, sinful, and God-dishonoring worldview. Consider the following text from the Old Testament law:

> Now if a person sins after he hears a public adjuration to testify when he is a witness, whether he has seen or otherwise known, if he does not tell it, then he will bear his guilt. Or if a person touches any unclean thing, whether a carcass of an unclean beast or the carcass of unclean cattle or a carcass of unclean swarming things though it is hidden from him and he is unclean, then he will be guilty. Or if he touches human uncleanness, of whatever sort his uncleanness may be with which he becomes unclean, and it is hidden from him, and then he comes to know it, he will be guilty. Or if a person swears thoughtlessly with his lips to do evil or to do good, in whatever matter a man may speak thoughtlessly with an oath, and it is hidden from him, and then he comes to know it, he will be guilty in one of these. So it shall be when he becomes guilty in one of these, that he shall confess that in which he has sinned. He shall also bring his guilt offering to the Lord for his sin which he has committed, a female from the flock, a lamb or a goat as a sin offering. So the priest shall make atonement on his behalf for his sin. (Leviticus 5:1–6)

Our point here is not to exposit the Old Testament law concerning guilt offerings. Rather, consider how this passage underscores our earlier point—that in Scripture we find the universal principle that sin is always very specific to and attributable to an individual. Sin is never vicarious, delegated, or accredited. Never. Look back at the end of the Leviticus passage and count the personal pronouns God uses in outlining for us when and how this law of guilt offerings is to be applied.

> So it shall be when *he* becomes guilty in one of these, that *he* shall confess that in which *he* has sinned. *He* shall also bring *his* guilt offering to the Lord for *his* sin which *he* has committed, a female from the flock, a lamb or a goat as a sin offering. So the priest shall make atonement on *his* behalf for *his* sin.

The point, again, is that sin is both specific *and* attributable. It is a principle clearly evident in the words of Paul in Romans 14:12, "So then each one of us will give an account of himself to God."

Another Old Testament text that teaches this same principle—that sin is specific and attributable, not vicarious or delegated—is found in 1 Samuel 20. There, David is on the run from King Saul, but Saul's son Jonathan is aiding David in his efforts to escape Saul's wrath. Chapter 20 begins, "Then David fled from Naioth in Ramah, and came and said to Jonathan, 'What have I done? What is my iniquity? And what is my sin before your father, that he is seeking my life?'" (v. 1).

It is important to note that in Hebrew, the word "before" is translated "against" or "upon." So, David is asking Jonathan—rhetorically, no doubt, because David knows in his heart that the answer to the question is "nothing"—"What is my iniquity? And what is my sin against or upon your father, that he is seeking my life?"

Did you catch that? David is asking Jonathan, "What is *my* personal sin I have committed before your father?" David is pleading with Jonathan to identify for him what specific sin he has committed against Saul to warrant Saul's seeking his life. These are the exact same questions we are asking of black evangelical pro-reparationists today: What specific sin has been committed against or upon you by white people that you are now seeking reparations from them? What have they done to you? You were never enslaved. So why would you deserve reparations?

Out of Step with Scripture

We must have the conversation within this context, considering what it is we believe any particular white person has done to require of them some kind of remuneration. We must ask questions like, "What is the end goal? What has a white person done to oppress you specifically? What is anyone white currently doing to hold you back from achieving a goal?" The answers to these kinds of questions really reveal that what we are discussing actually has nothing to do with what is currently happening. What we are really talking about is something that happened historically and, for the most part, has already been rectified by current law.

Christians should be willing to consider this issue in light of biblical principles. Our claim is that evangelical pro-reparationists are out of step with Scripture. It is those of us who are in Christ who have the ministry of reconciliation, and if our lens is clouded with something social justice–oriented, we will not be effective in seeing true change take place. It is wholly unbiblical and unchristian for a professing believer to see the world through race-colored glasses. Scripture is clear, objective, and unambiguous on this idea of sin being specific and attributable, not proximate and vicarious.

We find this principle again in John 19 in Jesus's second Roman trial as he stands before Pilate:

> Pilate then took Jesus and scourged Him. And the soldiers twisted together a crown of thorns and put it on His head, and put a purple robe on Him; and they began to come up to Him and say, "Hail, King of the Jews!" and to give Him slaps in the face. Pilate came out again and said to them, "Behold, I am bringing Him out to you so that you may know that I find no guilt in Him." Jesus then came out, wearing the crown of thorns and the purple robe. Pilate said to them, "Behold, the Man!" So when the chief priests and the officers saw Him, they cried out saying, "Crucify, crucify!" Pilate said to them, "Take Him yourselves and crucify Him, for I find no guilt in Him." The Jews answered him, "We have a law, and by that law He ought to die because He made Himself out to be the Son of God." (John 19:1–7)

Twice Pilate says of Jesus, "I find no guilt in Him." Here, again, we see the principle that sin is very specific and attributable. Now, we know that Jesus lived a sinless life. Nevertheless, the point here is that Pilate himself determined that there was no basis in Roman law for the charges being lodged against Jesus, as he could find no objective evidence that Jesus was personally guilty of what he was being accused of. Pilate said, "I find no guilt in Him." Sin is *always* specific and personal; it is *never* vicarious or "proximate."

The Poster Child for Reparations

This same principle is what many pro-reparationist Christians get wrong, for example, about Zaccheus in Luke 19:1–8, which is the go-to passage for many evangelical pro-reparationists who try to offer an apologetic for why reparations for slavery is biblical.

> He entered Jericho and was passing through. And there was a man called by the name of Zaccheus; he was a chief tax collector and he was rich. Zaccheus was trying to see who Jesus was, and was unable because of the crowd, for he was small in stature. So he ran on ahead and climbed up into a sycamore tree in order to see Him, for He was about to pass through that way. When Jesus came to the place, He looked up and said to him, "Zaccheus, hurry and come down, for today I must stay at your house." And he hurried and came down and received Him gladly. When they saw it, they all began to grumble, saying, "He has gone to be the guest of a man who is a sinner." Zaccheus stopped and said to the Lord, "Behold, Lord, half of my possessions I will give to the poor, and if I have defrauded anyone of anything, I will give back four times as much." (Luke 19:1–8)

We would like to propose several reasons why evangelical pro-reparationists are wrong about Zaccheus as it relates to the issue of reparations:

1. Zaccheus was a tax collector, not a slave owner (v. 2), therefore, whatever restitution that *would have been* warranted would have had to have been in accordance with the specific sin he would have committed in the carrying out of his duties as a tax collector. We see this same thing

when John the Baptist interacts with tax collectors in Luke 3:12–13: "And some tax collectors also came to be baptized, and they said to him, 'Teacher, what shall we do [to be saved]?' And he said to them, 'Collect no more than what you have been ordered to.'" It was this principle of honest collecting that Zaccheus was known to have violated among the people, which is why in Luke 19:7 the people described him as a "sinner."

2. Zaccheus's sin was personal, not proximate. Zaccheus says, "and if I have defrauded anyone" (v. 8). He personally sinned; it was not vicarious.

3. Zaccheus's volitional offer of restitution was the result of conversion, not coercion (v. 8).

4. The restitution Zaccheus offered would have come from his own personal possessions, not someone else's, such as the government. He said, "Half of my possessions I am giving to the poor" (v. 8). He didn't say, "the government's possessions"; he made restitution from what he personally owned.

5. The restitution Zaccheus offered was specific and applicable only to those who had actually been defrauded by him: "if I have extorted anything from anyone" (v. 8). To bring this directly to the topic of modern reparations, today no black person in the United States can accuse any white person in the United States of enslaving them. No white American today could say, "If I have enslaved anyone, I will make it right." It is not a reality today in the United States.

6. Only those of whom it could be objectively proven to have been defrauded by Zaccheus would have qualified to partake of his offer to "give back four times as much" to them (v. 8).

Zaccheus cannot be used as the poster child for an evangelical reparationist apologetic because he does not apply.

Politicizing Inequality

The truth is that what was propagated for centuries in total disregard of the universal principle of the *imago Dei* as recorded in Genesis 1:27, and rightly decried and denounced as an immoral practice, is today being leveraged by many professing Christians to materially enrich themselves. This is not on the objective basis of unjust suffering that they themselves actually experienced but on the backs of the unjust suffering experienced by others. In other words, you owe us money not because we suffered like people such as those from the slave narratives at the beginning of this chapter but because we look like them.

If you've not read Dr. Thomas Sowell's book *The Quest for Cosmic Justice*, we highly recommend that you do. Consider what he writes about the dangers of politicizing inequality:

> Equality, like justice, is one of the most fateful—and undefined—words of our time. Whole societies can be, and have been, jeopardized by the passionate pursuit of this elusive notion. There is nothing wrong with equality in itself. In fact, there is much that is attractive about the idea. At the very least, glaring inequities are unattractive, even for those who accept them as either inevitable, like death, or as the lesser of alternative evils. But to equate the attractiveness of the concept with a mandate for public policy aimed at equality is to assume that politicizing inequality is free of costs and dangers, when in fact such politicization can have very high costs and very grave dangers. The abstract desirability of equality, like the abstract desirability of immortality, is beside the point when choosing what practical course of action to follow. What matters is what we are prepared to do, to risk, or to sacrifice, in pursuit of what can turn out to be a mirage.[9]

Sowell raises an important question. What are we willing to risk in the pursuit of what may be a mirage?

Many brush off Sowell's warnings, instead claiming that dealing with inequality and injustice on a national scale will bring political and even spiritual healing. In June of 2014, *The Atlantic* published an article entitled "The Case for Reparations," written by a gentleman by

---

9 Thomas Sowell, *The Quest for Cosmic Justice* (New York: Touchstone, 1999), 51.

the name of Ta-Nehisi Coates, who serves as a national correspondent for the publication on matters of culture and politics. Coates's article was widely acclaimed for being one of the most erudite contemporary arguments for reparations made in recent years. But in the article Coates says the following: "Reparations—by which I mean the full acceptance of our collective biography and its consequences—is the price we must pay to see ourselves squarely. . . . What I'm talking about is more than recompense for past injustices—more than a handout, a payoff, hush money, or a reluctant bribe. What I'm talking about is a national reckoning that would lead to spiritual renewal."[10]

There are several things we find problematic with Coates's thinking. What does Coates mean by "acceptance of our collective biography"? America's "collective biography" is its history as a nation, and sadly, slavery is a significant part of that history. It does not need to be "accepted," as Coates suggests; it is history. And as history is inherently immutable, it can neither be "accepted" or "rejected." It simply is. And who is the representative or board we go to in order to certify that our collective biography has now been accepted? Where do we find them? In reality, this is merely empty language employed for the purpose of sounding erudite but actually is just a massive virtue signal that means nothing.

Further, what does Coates mean by seeing ourselves "squarely"? Against what objective ethical or moral standard or definition will it be determined that we, as a collective nation, have attained to this "square" view of ourselves with regard to slavery? By what objective metrics would such a goal be determined to have been achieved, and conversely, what subsequently would come next, if anything, and who would possess the authority to determine what that next step is?

To assume that the payment of reparations—whether viewed as a "payoff," "hush money," or a "reluctant bribe"—would lead to a collective "national reckoning" is naïve and presumptive. Such reasoning is rooted in the presupposition that we all hold to the same ethical and moral paradigm to begin with, which we know is not the

---

10 Ta-Nehisi Coates, "The Case for Reparations," *The Atlantic*, June 1, 2014, https://www.theatlantic.com/magazine/archive/2014/06/the-case-for-reparations/361631.

case. In the absence of an objective standard, whatever amount is determined will seem to one person not enough and to another, too much. You can see how quickly such thinking just gets silly. Beyond the sheer absurdity is the sobering reality that such a rationale places a price tag on that which can only be accomplished by the Spirit of God in a person's heart.

The bottom line here is that political candidates and those who support the idea of reparations really believe that black people are stupid. They use language that they know elicits emotion for the purpose of obtaining power. Essentially, *reparations* is just the new forty acres and a mule.

Racism and Reparations

This leaves us with a concerning final question: What is the motivation of evangelical pro-reparationists? Is it anything more than an empty virtue signal on their part? We understand what political candidates are trying to gain, but for these evangelicals, of what benefit is it in their view?

To put it bluntly, there are a lot of evangelical reparationists out there who are black and who are racist. They are racist in their hearts. While the term *racist* isn't a biblical one, its cultural significance makes it useful in our discussion. When we say that there are black evangelicals who claim to be Christian and are racist, what we mean is that they hate white people. They certainly won't come out and admit that, but their actions and words show they hate them. That hatred is the answer to the question regarding their motivation in the push for reparations. The words of the apostle John in 1 John 4:20 condemn them: "If someone says, 'I love God,' and hates his brother, he is a liar; for the one who does not love his brother whom he has seen, cannot love God whom he has not seen." Where ethnic prejudice (racism) exists in the church, there must be confession and repentance of that sin, for it is nothing less than the sin of hatred (1 John 2:9-11).

We want to end our discussion on reparations by again quoting from Dr. Thomas Sowell's book *Discrimination and Disparities*, which offers a solid antithesis to the pro-reparationist apologetic of people like Ta-Nehisi Coates and others who share his perspective on this issue. Sowell writes this:

> Such wrongs abound in times and places around the world—inflicted on, and perpetrated by, people of virtually every race, creed, and color. But what can any society today hope to gain by having newborn babies in that society enter the world as heirs to prepackaged grievances against other babies born into that same society on the same day?
>
> Nothing that we can do today can undo the many evils and catastrophes of the past, but we can at least learn from them, and not repeat the mistakes of the past, many of which began with lofty-sounding goals. Obvious as all this might seem, it is too often forgotten. Nothing that Germans can do today will in any way mitigate the staggering evils of what Hitler did in the past. Nor can apologies in America today for slavery in the past have any meaning, much less do any good, for either blacks or whites today. What can it mean for "A" to apologize for what "B" did, even among contemporaries, much less across the vast chasm between the living and the dead?
>
> The only times over which we have any degree of influence at all are the present and the future—both of which can be made worse by attempts at symbolic restitution among the living for what happened among the dead, who are far beyond our power to help or punish or avenge. Galling as these restrictive facts may be, that does not stop them from being facts beyond our control. Pretending to have powers that we do not in fact have risks creating needless evils in the present, while claiming to deal with the evils of the past.
>
> Any serious consideration of the world as it is around us today must tell us that maintaining common decency, much less peace and harmony, among living contemporaries is a major challenge, both among nations and within nations. To admit that we can do nothing about what happened among the dead is not to give up the struggle for a better world, but to concentrate our efforts where they have at least some hope of making things better for the living.[11]

---

11 Sowell, *Discrimination*, 222–223.

Discussion Questions

1. When discussing reparations, it's important to have a clear-eyed view of what happened. We opened this chapter with slave narratives. How were you impacted by the stories?

2. We cannot stop at the shores of North America when discussing reparations. As Darrell explains his background, why is that critical in a discussion about reparations?

3. Why are Deuteronomy 24:16 and Ezekiel 18:19–22, two texts we referenced, important to a discussion about reparations?

4. Why is the story of Zacchaeus a bad example for pro-reparations evangelicals to use?

5. Why is understanding the doctrine of total depravity vital to the discussion about reparations?

The Equality Act

Twentieth-century British historian Arnold J. Toynbee spent much of his academic life studying the rise and fall of human civilizations. Over the course of twenty-seven years, from 1934 to 1961, Toynbee published a twelve-volume series entitled *A Study of History*. Toynbee's goal in *A Study of History* was to trace the development and decay of nineteen world civilizations, detailing the five stages through which all great societies and civilizations pass:

Stage 1: Genesis

Stage 2: Growth

Stage 3: Times of Trouble

Stage 4: The Universal State

Stage 5: Disintegration

According to Toynbee, civilizations start to decay when they lose their moral fiber. It was that reality that prompted Toynbee to conclude that "civilizations die from suicide, not murder."[1]

---

1 Arnold J. Toynbee, *The Story of History: Abridgement of Volumes I-VI*, Abridgement by D. C. Somerville (New York: Oxford University Press, 1957), 2:273.

What exactly does Toynbee mean by "moral fiber"? Where does mankind get the idea of moral fiber to begin with? Well, we know from Scripture that this moral fiber, as Toynbee termed it, is inherent in every human being. We see this in Romans 1: "For the wrath of God is revealed from heaven against all ungodliness and unrighteousness of men who suppress the truth in unrighteousness, because that which is known about God is evident within them, for God made it evident to them. For since the creation of the world His invisible attributes, His eternal power and divine nature, have been clearly seen, being understood through what has been made, so that they are without excuse" (Romans 1:18–20).

Now, lest we forget, the pronoun "they" at the end of verse 20, to whom this moral fiber has been imparted by God, includes every human being who has ever been born. And when we "suppress the truth in unrighteousness," civilization begins to decay. It is a direct result of hating God and loving our sin. The natural depravity of the human heart lends itself to what we see being played out in society.

John MacArthur, in his book *The Battle for the Beginning*, expounds on that point, saying:

> When God made us in His image, He made us as persons, that is, He made us for having relationships, particularly with Him. It is impossible to divorce this truth from the fact that man is an ethical creature. All true relationships have ethical ramifications. And it is at this point that God's communicable attributes come into play—marred though our moral and ethical sense may be because of humanity's fall into sin. We still know right from wrong in a basic sense. Even the most determined atheists still understand the concept of virtue and the need for morality. In fact, an inherent aspect of true humanity is moral sensibility. We know instinctively that there is a difference between good and evil.[2]

So, in Romans 1 the apostle Paul, without ambiguity, is declaring "that which is known about God"—and the phrase "known about

---

2 John MacArthur, *The Battle for the Beginning* (Nashville: Thomas Nelson, 2012), 165.

God" includes an awareness of God's equitable standards of right and wrong—is evident within each of us and that those principles and precepts are evident within us because God himself has made them evident within us. That reality is what is referred to in Christian theology as *natural revelation* or *general revelation*.

We see the idea of God's natural revelation expressed in the words of Psalm 19:1: "The heavens are telling of the glory of God; and their expanse is declaring the work of His hands." That God has revealed himself in creation is why, at the end of the day, no one can be a true atheist, because natural revelation is so clear. John Calvin emphasized that point in his *Institutes of the Christian Religion*, where he said, "[God's] essence, indeed, is incomprehensible, utterly transcending all human thought; but on each of his works his glory is engraven in characters so bright, so distinct, and so illustrious, that none, however dull and illiterate, can plead ignorance as their excuse."[3]

So, Scripture is clear that none of us has an excuse to disregard the God-ordained boundaries within which he has ordained we should live. And yet, in the stubbornness of our hearts, we continue to pride ourselves on doing exactly that, disregarding God's righteous precepts and principles for how we are to live and conduct ourselves in this world.

In *Revelation and God*, volume 1 of *Reformed Systematic Theology*, Joel R. Beeke and Paul M. Smalley expound on the implications of creation and revelation to man: "Man is part of God's creation; indeed, he is the pinnacle of God's works on earth (Genesis 1). Therefore, God's general revelation through his created works also shines through the human race, and that in a heightened manner. Just as God's creation of man involved the image of God and man's moral obligation to obey God's law (Genesis 1:26–28; 2:15–17), so general revelation in man involves our image bearing and inner sense of divine obligation and accountability."[4]

---

3 John Calvin, *Institutes of the Christian Religion*, trans. Robert White (Edinburgh: Banner of Truth, 2014), 1.5.1.
4 Joel R. Beeke and Paul M. Smalley, *Reformed Systematic Theology* (Wheaton, IL: Crossway, 2019), 1:201.

As image-bearers of God, we are keenly aware of him and of his attributes, righteousness, righteous laws, judgments, and decrees. But we have determined that we are going to subjugate that knowledge because we love our sin. One of the most egregious examples of society's repeated attempts to disregard what Beeke and Smalley referred to as our "obligation and accountability" to God is in our incessant efforts to normalize the sin we love, particularly the sin of homosexuality. Our society has specifically and repeatedly tried to do this through federal legislation—that is, by enacting the normalization of sin into law so that any attempts to resist those efforts to legalize such sinful behavior are made subject to heavily punitive and retaliatory responses. A recent example of this is the Equality Act of 2019.[5]

Now, the reason we must be specific in referring to this legislation as the Equality Act of 2019 is because this isn't the first time Congress has attempted to pass this kind of legislation into law. In fact, as far back as nearly half a century ago, in 1974, a liberal Democrat congresswoman from New York, Bella S. Abzug, introduced H.R. 14752, referred to then as the Equality Act, which, like the Equality Act of 2019, proposed to "prohibit, under the Civil Rights Act of 1964, discrimination on account of sex, marital status or sexual orientation in places of public accommodation, and under color of State law. Provides for civil actions by the Attorney General where there is discrimination on account of sex, marital status, or sexual orientation in public facilities or in public education."[6]

Fast forward to today, and the language of the Equality Act of 2019, known also as H.R. 5, not only mirrors the language of the bill proposed forty-five years ago—it goes much further in its application:

> This bill prohibits discrimination based on sex, sexual orientation, and gender identity in areas including public accommodations and facilities, education, federal funding, employment, housing, credit, and the jury system. Specifically, the bill defines and includes sex, sexual orientation, and gender identity among the

---

5 The Equality Act of 2019 stopped at the House in the 116th Cong. Though there is a new duplicate H.R. 5 in the 117th Cong., introduced on 2/18/21 and passed by the House on 2/25/21, we refer to the original of 2019 here.
6 Equality Act, H. R. 15742, 93rd Cong. (1974).

prohibited categories of discrimination or segregation. The bill expands the definition of public accommodations to include places or establishments that provide (1) exhibitions, recreation, exercise, amusement, gatherings, or displays; (2) goods, services, or programs; and (3) transportation services. The bill allows the Department of Justice to intervene in equal protection actions in federal court on account of sexual orientation or gender identity. The bill prohibits an individual from being denied access to a shared facility, including a restroom, a locker room, and a dressing room, that is in accordance with the individual's gender identity.[7]

It is that last sentence, particularly the words "in accordance with the individual's gender identity," that makes the Equality Act of 2019 so dangerous. It is dangerous not only because of the intrinsic and deliberate ambiguity of that language but also because the whole idea of "gender identity" is a rejection of what Scripture clearly teaches in Genesis 1:27: "God created man in His own image, in the image of God He created him; *male and female* He created them" (emphasis added).

The idea of gender identity is evidence of how sin has so affected our hearts and minds that apart from Christ our nature and our way of thinking is exactly as the apostle John describes in John 3:19–20: "This is the judgment, that the Light has come into the world, and men loved the darkness rather than the Light; for their deeds were evil. For everyone who does evil hates the Light, and does not come to the Light for fear that his deeds will be exposed." The apostle Paul explains why that is in Romans 8:6–8: "For the mind set on the flesh is death, but the mind set on the Spirit is life and peace, because the mind set on the flesh is hostile toward God; for it does not subject itself to the law of God, for it is not even able to do so, and those who are in the flesh cannot please God."

Second Thessalonians 2:11–12 gives us the consequences of hearts that hate the Light and minds that are hostile toward God: "For this reason God will send upon them a deluding influence so that they will believe what is false, in order that they all may be judged who did not

---

[7] Equality Act, H. R. 5, 116th Cong. (2019); 117th Cong. (2021).

believe the truth, but took pleasure in wickedness." The very fact that the Equality Act of 2019 exists is because there are people who do not believe the truth about God's design for men and women and instead take pleasure in wickedness.

There is such foolishness in the wording of this act, particularly in the prohibition against segregation on the basis of sex. We purpose to segregate on the basis of our sex. Why? Because we're different. We have different body parts, and there should be protection, particularly for young women around young men. To ignore that is to ignore reality.

Furthermore, by basing determination on "the individual's gender identity," the Equality Act codifies sin into law for the purpose of establishing the pseudo-religious anthropology of secular humanism. It is crazy to establish law based on an inherently unstable individual emotional state. It is a complete rejection of God's established standard and mirrors what Satan did in Genesis 3, asking, "Did God really say?" That question establishes doubt of God's standard, and the lawmakers who support this act are doing exactly what Romans 1:18 says the ungodly do, "suppress the truth in unrighteousness." Ecclesiastes 9:3 sums up what is happening: "This is an evil in all that is done under the sun, that there is one fate for all men. Furthermore, the hearts of the sons of mankind are full of evil and insanity is in their hearts throughout their lives."

Historical Reality: The Civil Rights Act

Like its previous iterations, the Equality Act of 2019 is attempting to leverage (or, more accurately, hijack) the Civil Rights Act of 1964. But the Civil Rights Act of 1964 was based on objective and universal truth, *not* subjective, abstract, and suppositious realities. The Civil Rights Act outlawed discrimination on the basis of race, color, religion, sex, or national origin. It mandated equal access to public places and employment and enforced desegregation of schools and the right to vote.

The National Park Service, whose history was greatly impacted by segregation, offers an excellent summary of the conditions the Civil Rights Act was designed to address:

> Although the 13th, 14th, and 15th amendments to the United States Constitution [the Reconstruction Amendments] outlawed slavery, provided for equal protection under the law, guaranteed citizenship, and protected the right to vote, individual states continued to allow unfair treatment of blacks and passed Jim Crow laws allowing segregation of public facilities. These were upheld by the Supreme Court in Plessy v. Ferguson (1895), which found state laws requiring racial segregation that were "separate but equal" to be constitutional. This finding helped continue legalized discrimination well into the 20th century.[8]

In addition to Jim Crow laws, there also were the Black Codes, strict laws detailing when, where, and how freed slaves could work and for how much compensation. The codes appeared throughout the South as a legal way to put black citizens into indentured servitude, to take voting rights away, to control where they lived and how they traveled, and to seize their children for purposes of manual labor.

As if Jim Crow and the Black Codes weren't enough, there was the little-known post-Reconstruction peonage system. *Peonage*, also called "debt slavery" or "debt servitude," is a system in which an employer would compel a worker to pay off a debt with labor. Legally, peonage was outlawed by Congress in 1867. However, after Reconstruction, many Southern black men were swept into peonage though different methods, and the system was not completely eradicated until the 1940s.

In the South, many black men were picked up for minor crimes and infractions or on trumped-up charges and, when faced with staggering fines and court fees, forced to work for a local employer, who would pay their fines for them. Southern states also leased their convicts en mass to local industrialists. The paperwork and debt record of individual prisoners were often lost, and these men found themselves

---

8 "Civil Rights Act of 1964," National Park Service, accessed May 20, 2021, https://www.nps.gov/articles/civil-rights-act.htm.

trapped in inescapable situations. It is the peonage system that gave rise to the term *peon*.[9]

Immutable and Fixed

We are not taking the time to give this history lesson in order to resurrect the injustices of black people in America. God knows there are enough people doing that already without our helping them out. Instead, our purpose here is to establish that what primarily influenced the legislative remedies put in place to right such injustices as slavery, Jim Crow, the Black Codes, and peonage was a realization that equality was inherent to our common identity as human beings who possess certain fixed and immutable characteristics such as ethnicity and sex.

An example of this is that during the Civil Rights movement of the 1960s, many black men would be seen walking in circles in front of restaurants or other establishments that refused to serve black customers, wearing "sandwich-board" signs. These sandwich-board signs were two-sided placards you would put on over your head, and they would rest on your shoulders so you could walk around with them. On each side of the sign it read, in all caps, "I AM A MAN."

The signs didn't read, "I AM A BLACK MAN," or "I AM A MARGINALIZED MAN," or "I IDENTIFY AS A MAN." No, the signs simply read, "I AM A MAN." In those four short words, those protesters were making the case for Genesis 1:27 in that they, like their white counterparts, were also created in the image of God and that *on that basis alone* were deserving of equal treatment under federal and state law. God's natural law, which is inherent to every human being, as we saw previously in Romans 1, required it.

The problem with the Equality Act of 2019 is that LGBTQ people cannot make that same argument from Genesis 1:27 and, therefore, cannot claim that gender identity and sexual orientation are matters of "civil rights." Unlike ethnicity and sex, orientation and identity are mutable and changeable, not immutable and fixed.

---

9 For more information on the peonage system, see Douglas A. Blackmon, *Slavery by Another Name: The Re-Enslavement of Black Americans from the Civil War to World War II*.

Though the Equality Act of 2019 describes itself as "expanding on the Civil Rights Act of 1964," what it is really attempting to do is write into law preferential rights based *not* on the common immutable attributes we all share as image-bearers of God. Rather, the Equality Act yields to the subjective and mutable whims, impulses, and inclinations of an extremely small group of people who have convinced themselves and others that it is possible, and even normal, to morph from one "identity" or "orientation" to another. This group seeks with impunity to force others to recognize and accommodate their choice of identity or orientation under the threat of severe penalties for not doing so.

But our world is not an ice cream shop where you have thirty-one "flavors" of sexual orientation or gender. No, God's Word declares that there are only two: male and female.

The Prostitution of the Civil Rights Act of 1964

The Civil Rights Act of 1964 was not a theological document, to be sure, but its key tenets were grounded in the universal principle that equality is a matter of the immutable characteristics we each possess as image-bearers of God. Because of this foundation, the Civil Rights Act did not set up special status or additional rights for some based on a standard that did not apply equally to all. In 1851, Sojourner Truth delivered one of the most famous abolitionist speeches, in which she declared, "Aint I a Woman?" Her argument was based on those immutable characteristics, and her desire was to be treated by the same standard as all men and women regardless of their color. She appealed to no subjective, emotional, ever-changing standard but to the objective standard of being a woman.

Attributes such as ethnicity and sex are immutable characteristics that apply to every human being. But the Equality Act of 2019 is based on the absurd and ridiculous notion that those characteristics, particularly sexual orientation and gender identity, are in fact mutable and changeable. Interestingly, this represents a shift in the argument on homosexuality. It wasn't that long ago that the anthem of the LGBTQ movement was Lady Gaga's "I Was Born This

Way," as proponents claimed that sexual orientation was inborn and unchanging. Now, however, advocates of the LGBTQ lifestyle make the argument that you can wake up one morning and be more masculine or more feminine simply based on your feelings on that day. When you believe your emotional state determines what gender you are, accepting the concept of multiple genders and gender fluidity naturally follows.

The manner in which the Civil Rights Act of 1964 is being prostituted under the pretense of granting "civil rights" to a group of individuals who, in terms of numbers, are a significant minority in America should stir up righteous indignation within every professing Christian who is concerned about the granting of *legitimate* civil rights in this nation. The reality is that these individuals already enjoy all the civil rights granted to citizens of the United States. With this hijacking of the Civil Rights Act of 1964, the LGBTQ lobby is attempting to use the legislative process to coerce society, and especially Christians, to not only accept as normative their abnormal lifestyle choices but to bow down and submit to them.

The Danger of the Equality Act

It is not merely the two of us who recognize the danger and insanity of the Equality Act. Consider the following perspectives on the act from various national sources.

The Heritage Foundation, answering the question, "How Could Sexual Orientation and Gender Identity (SOGI) Laws Affect You?" writes, "Where the original Civil Rights Act of 1964 furthered equality by ensuring that African Americans had equal access to public accommodations and material goods, the Equality Act would further inequality by penalizing everyday Americans for their beliefs about marriage and biological sex. Similar sexual orientation and gender identity laws at the state and local level have already been used in this way."[10]

---

10 "Heritage Explains the Equality Act," The Heritage Foundation, accessed May 20, 2021, https://www.heritage.org/gender/heritage-explains/the-equality-act.

In the article "The Equality Act is a Time Bomb," *National Review* warned, "The sweeping legislation would amend the Civil Rights Act of 1964 to include sexual orientation and gender identity as protected characteristics. But it goes further than that. Under the guise of anti-discrimination protections, the bill redefines sex to include gender identity, undermines religious freedom, gives males who identify as females the right to women's spaces, and sets a dangerous political precedent for the medicalization of gender-confused youth."[11]

Human Events author Doreen Denny points out that "The 'Equality Act' is a Danger to American Women":

> This legislation has no rules about what constitutes a legitimate claim to "gender identity" as a protected class. Any male (or female) can claim identity as the opposite sex without proof of medical diagnosis or permanent intent. Sex-based identity is completely subjective and determined by perception or desire and can be changed at any time.
>
> Society's purpose for sex-segregation, a major factor of women's safety, is negated under this legislation. Women could no longer claim rights to our safety and equal protections because men could claim our rights just by claiming to be women. Perhaps the sponsor of this bill, a gay man, doesn't understand our concerns. Women are safer in places they know men can't legitimately access.
>
> If this bill passes, men, go ahead, put on your makeup and take a walk in a women's locker room for a day. You don't have to prove anything, just claim your feminine side. Women would be commanded to open the door to any female-posing male who wants access to women's sex-specific spaces.[12]

In "The inequality of the Equality Act," Mary Beth Waddell of the *Washington Times* writes, "The In-Equality Act, unfortunately, isn't about equality at all. Rather, it's about government-imposed ideology

---

[11] Madeleine Kearns, "The Equality Act Is a Time Bomb," *National Review*, May 20, 2019, https://www.nationalreview.com/corner/the-equality-act-is-a-time-bomb.
[12] Doreen Duffy, "The 'Equality Act' Is a Danger to American Women," Human Events, accessed March 26, 2021, https://humanevents.com/2019/05/14/the-equality-act-is-a-danger-to-american-women/?utm_referrer=https%3A%2F%2Fwww.bing.com%2F.

and unfairness. When discussing her agenda for this Congress, House Speaker Nancy Pelosi said, 'if there is some collateral damage for some others who do not share our view so be it.'"[13]

Finally, here's what conservative political activist Star Parker had to say about the Equality Act: "Civil rights law was designed to protect human dignity by preventing individuals from being reduced to pre-existing realities not connected to their personal choices, such as ethnicity. Now with this law, the sexual behavior they choose, and the sex they decide they are, will receive the same protections. We must vigilantly fight to prevent this legislation from passing into law."[14]

Politics: A Means to an End

We are witnessing the recreating of humanity into the image of humanism. Feelings have been elevated to the throne of worship, and it has been determined that the text of this new orthodoxy will be codified into law by the government. Violators will be punished, so you must bow the knee and genuflect to the whims of the new prophets, the politicians in Washington. As Christians, we must wake up and do something about this.

At its most fundamental level, what we are being confronted with here is a matter not of politics but worldview. That's not to say that politics is not a factor in our discussion about the Equality Act of 2019 because, most assuredly, it is a factor and not an insignificant one. After all, politics is the means being used to implement an anti-biblical worldview. The unfortunate truth is that there are many who profess to be Christian today who helped elect to office many of the men and women in Congress who are supporting this piece of ungodly legislation, and whom God himself will hold accountable one day for doing so. We believe that, for Christians, it is both a responsibility and obligation to elect believers to office so as to guard against this kind of anti-God, anti-Christ, and anti-Christian legislation.

---

13 Mary Beth Waddell, "The inequality of the Equality Act," *The Washington Times*, May 15, 2019, https://www.washingtontimes.com/news/2019/may/15/the-inequality-of-the-equality-act.
14 Star Parker, "The Suicidal Equality Act of 2019," *The Patriot Post*, June 26, 2019, https://patriotpost.us/opinion/62862-the-suicidal-equality-act-of-2019.

Consider the words of an eighteenth-century Presbyterian theologian by the name of George Duffield, who said,

> For a society of professing Christians to agree to employ none in any of their principal offices of service in the State but such as profess Christianity, appears to be no more than a proper mark of respect paid to themselves, as a body, and to the Christian religion they profess, and cannot therefore, in that point of view be condemned. . . . Good morals are essentially necessary to the health and prosperity of the State. Whatever measure, therefore, appears best adapted to preserve and promote the morals of the State ought to be embraced. Christianity is much better calculated to preserve and promote good morals than infidelity; as much, therefore, as Christianity is better calculated for this great essential purpose, so much more advisable and prudent it is to have Christian magistrates and officers rather than infidels.[15]

In light of Duffield's comments, it is interesting to think about how much political campaigning has changed in recent years. Many of today's career politicians started out decades ago advertising the fact that they were Christians or Catholics, willingly stating what they believed. Then came qualifications such as "I'm a Catholic, but I won't allow my Catholic upbringing to inform my political preferences." Today we see an even greater shift to wanting to affirm that which is anti-biblical through supporting LGBTQ lifestyles. It is such a clear attempt to banish any expression of Christian belief from the public eye.

Further back in church history, we find the Belgic Confession (c. 1561), a Reformed confession of the Dutch churches. Article 36 of the confession says this regarding the role of "The Magistracy," or Civil Government:

> We believe that because of the depravity of the human race our good God has ordained kings, princes, and civil officers. He wants the world to be governed by laws and policies so that human lawlessness may be restrained and that everything may be conducted in good order among human beings. For that

---

15 R. Andrew Myers, "George Duffield Asks, 'Who Should Be Our Rulers?'" Log College Press, May 23, 2019, https://www.logcollegepress.com/blog/2019/5/21/george-duffield-asks-who-should-be-our-rulers.

purpose he has placed the sword in the hands of the government, to punish evil people and protect the good. And being called in this manner to contribute to the advancement of a society that is pleasing to God, the civil rulers have the task, subject to God's law, of removing every obstacle to the preaching of the gospel and to every aspect of divine worship. They should do this while completely refraining from every tendency toward exercising absolute authority, and while functioning in the sphere entrusted to them, with the means belonging to them. And the government's task is not limited to caring for and watching over the public domain but extends also to upholding the sacred ministry, with a view to removing and destroying all idolatry and false worship of the Antichrist; to promoting the kingdom of Jesus Christ; and to furthering the preaching of the gospel everywhere; to the end that God may be honored and served by everyone, as he requires in his Word.[16]

Make no mistake. The Equality Act of 2019, if passed into law, will be what the Belgic Confession described as an "obstacle to the preaching of the gospel" because the gospel preaches against the kinds of behavior that legislation seeks to normalize.

The Spiritual Element

Beyond the politics of the Equality Act of 2019, a distinct and tangible spiritual element is involved here in that the Equality Act arrogantly and unrepentantly denies God's created order for mankind. Recall the actual wording of the act: "An individual shall not be denied access to a shared facility, including a restroom, a locker room, and a dressing room, that is in accordance with *the individual's gender identity*."[17]

"The individual's gender identity"? You can't get any more ambiguous than that. But the ambiguity of that language is deliberate. The Equality Act of 2019 is a blatant, audacious, and unarguable rejection of Genesis 1:27. Theologian and cultural apologist Dr. Peter Jones has written a penetrating and revealing book entitled *One or*

---

16 "Article 36: Of Magistrates," Belgic Confession of Faith, Protestant Reformed Churches in America (PRCA), March 18, 2013, http://www.prca.org/about/official-standards/creeds/three-forms-of-unity/belgic-confession/article-36.
17 Equality Act, H.R. 5 (emphasis added).

Two: Seeing a World of Difference, in which he refers to this rejection of Genesis 1:27 as "neo-paganism":

> Western culture, often called Christendom, is being hijacked by a spiritual ideology that I call neo-paganism. . . . As a culture, we have largely freed ourselves of any restraining notions of God the Creator, but when we need civic pomposity, we claim "to hold these truths to be self-evident." We recite our official documents of yester-year, proclaiming that our "rights" are "endowed by the Creator." This disjunction between our past and present creates the great moment for religious paganism to take political and social power. Christianity as a social force is on the decline. Now that postmodernism has finished its blitzkrieg, people are hoping for a savior to clear the rubble. Neo-pagans are the darlings of a variety of movements. They lead the way in the "green" movement, in systems of wealth redistribution, in planetary programs for social justice, in solutions to global warming, in inter-faith conferences, in the normalization of sexual expressions, and in the promotion of globalist theories through the United Nations (UN). Kernels of truth in these theories give politicians and power brokers an excuse to seize power.[18]

Dr. Jones is absolutely correct. What the Equality Act of 2019 is attempting to pass off as "kernels of truth" is the lie that a person's volitional, subjective, and changeable decisions about sexual orientation and gender identity are deserving of the same civil rights protections as people for whom such rights are determined on the basis of fixed, objective, and unchangeable characteristics of personhood sovereignly determined by God from the moment of conception. In other words, the act proposes to grant civil rights to people not on the basis of attributes and characteristics of their humanity in which they had no choice (such as ethnicity and sex) but on the basis of self-determined choices about who and what they deem themselves to be.

The Equality Act of 2019, and all its preceding iterations, is nothing less than neo-paganism camouflaged as civil rights. And, as Christians, we need to be discerning enough to recognize this legislation for what

---

18 Peter Jones, *One or Two: Seeing a World of Difference* (Escondido, CA: Main Entry Editions, 2010), 9.

it is: yet another attempt by the federal government to target Christians by forcing them to submit to a law that promotes and endeavors to normalize the very sin that God himself prohibits.

Dr. Jones offers this insight: "Queer theory insists that 'all sexual behaviors and identities, and all categories of normative and deviant sexualities, are social constructs, [rejecting] the idea that sexuality is an essentialist category determined by biology or judged by external standards of morality and truth.' For this to happen, though, the key eternal standard of what is good and what is evil has to go. The truth to be overcome is moral."[19]

The truth that must be overcome is moral truth. In other words, the truth that must be replaced is the universal truth of Romans 1, that the knowledge of God and of his standard of right and wrong is inherent in each of us as image-bearers of God. It is that moral truth that must be replaced with a new moral truth—namely, that self-determining one's sexual orientation and gender identity is normal and acceptable.

As we said previously, this is the creation of a new orthodoxy, a rewriting of Scripture, and the establishment of a lie in the place of truth. John 3 is right; people love darkness rather than light, and they love it so much they want to write legislation that penalizes those who point out that it's dark. As Jeremiah 17:9 says, "The heart is more deceitful than all else and is desperately sick; who can understand it?"

The Equality Act of 2019 is the by-product of a society and culture which, as Dr. Peter Jones said, revels in sticking its depraved finger in God's holy eye. We Christians are not blameless in this. To a great degree, we are culpable that this kind of legislation even exists. We cannot dissociate ourselves from what is happening in our culture as if we had nothing to do with it.

How Will the Church React?

If the Equality Act of 2019 becomes law, many of the freedoms we, as Christians, enjoy in this nation will be lost, perhaps forever. Again,

---

19 Peter Jones, *The Other Worldview: Exposing Christianity's Greatest Threat* (Bellingham, WA: Kirkdale, 2015), 62.

the words of Dr. Jones are helpful here in challenging us to grasp the seriousness of what is happening in our society today: "Faced with unprecedented opposition to the Christian faith—a faith which was once the dominant source of social and moral definitions in Western culture—the response of believers is crucial for the very survival of the gospel in our day. This is a time unparalleled since the beginning of the history of the church, when religious paganism ruled the culture. Will the present church see the true nature of this situation and react in a way that honors Christ and his gospel—as the early church did?"[20]

This is a powerful question Dr. Jones poses. Too often the church seems to be in a reactionary stance to what is happening in the culture around us. We tend to neglect the first phrase of 1 Peter 3:15—"But in your hearts honor Christ the Lord as holy"—as the foundation from which we are called to be prepared "to make a defense to everyone who asks you to give an account for the hope that is in you." Some of us have been ready to defend the faith, but on the basis of politics or in support of a particular politician or in defense of an ideological position that has nothing to do with honoring Christ the Lord as holy. We must be prepared to honor Christ, willing even to give our lives if necessary for the sake of advancing the gospel of God.

In his book *The Truth War: Fighting for Christianity in an Age of Deception,* John MacArthur considers what is facing the church today:

> When it comes to biblical issues, moral principles, theological truth, divine revelation, and other spiritual absolutes, compromise is never appropriate. The church, caught up in the spirit of the age, is losing sight of that reality. The modern canonization of compromise represents a detour down a dead-end alley. Both Scripture and church history reveal the danger of compromising biblical truth. Those whom God uses are invariably men and women who swim against the tide. They hold strong convictions with great courage and refuse to compromise in the face of incredible opposition.
>
> Where are the men and women today with the courage to stand alone? The church in our age has abandoned the confrontive

---

20 Jones, 132.

stance. Instead of overturning worldly wisdom with revealed truth, many Christians today are obsessed with finding areas of agreement. The goal has become integration rather than confrontation. As the church absorbs the values of secular culture, it is losing its ability to differentiate between good and evil. What will happen to the church if everyone proceeds down the slippery slope of public opinion?[21]

To a great extent, Americanized Christianity is a Christianity that has grown fat and lazy. The words of Arnold Toynbee are a warning: "Civilizations die from suicide, not murder."

While we Christians have been busy fighting among ourselves over such issues as complementarianism and social justice, we've become oblivious to the deliberately clandestine and surreptitious efforts of individuals and institutions outside the body of Christ to render Christianity, and the gospel, subordinate to a neo-pagan sociocultural worldview. That is exactly what the Equality Act of 2019 desires to accomplish.

And if that legislation passes into law, may God forgive us for our laziness and apathy and for wasting our time and energy waging war with one another instead of with those who are the true enemies of Christ and his church.

Discussion Questions

1. The language "equality act" is a misnomer. Why?
2. According to Toynbee, what are the five stages of the decay of a great nation? Where are we in that process?
3. What does Romans 1 have to say about a culture that ignores God?
4. Did the civil rights bill of 1964 provide special rights or equal rights? What's the difference?
5. How is the Equality Act a special right?

---

21 John MacArthur, *The Truth War: Fighting for Christianity in an Age of Deception* (Nashville: Thomas Nelson, 2007), 192.

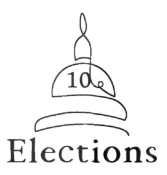

Elections

As this book is nearing completion in December of 2020, we in the United States are in the midst of a prolonged election cycle in which, only a few of weeks ago, tens of millions of Americans, many professing to be Christians, cast their vote for candidates running for elected offices ranging from state and local positions to president and vice president of the United States. As with previous election cycles, this year's election is full of issues and has become an extremely contentious, divisive, and alienating affair, to the extent that some relationships within the church are being fractured and, in certain instances, torn apart altogether.

As followers of Jesus Christ, we might expect that politics would have that kind of effect on relationships built on the ever-shifting and unstable foundations of the world but not on relationships that are supposedly founded on the firm and eternal principles and precepts of the Word of God. However, even those of us who claim the name of Jesus Christ are not immune to succumbing to the trappings, temptations, and enticements of this passing world, and politics can definitely be one of the things that has the potential to strain and even destroy the relationships we have with others who are within the body of Christ.

It shouldn't be that way, of course, but it often is. And it happens largely because our affections are misplaced. The New Testament gives us insight into this issue:

> Do not love the world nor the things in the world. If anyone loves the world, the love of the Father is not in him. For all that is in the world, the lust of the flesh and the lust of the eyes and the boastful pride of life, is not from the Father, but is from the world. The world is passing away, and also its lusts, but the one who does the will of God lives forever. (1 John 2:15–17)

> Therefore if you have been raised up with Christ, keep seeking the things above, where Christ is, seated at the right hand of God. Set your mind on the things above, not on the things that are on earth. For you have died and your life is now hidden with Christ in God. (Colossians 3:1–3)

When we allow the affections to be misplaced, permitting our hearts and minds to be so enamored with the things of the world (including politics) that we are drawn away from what the apostle Paul describes in 1 Corinthians 15:3 as those things that are "of first importance," our relationship with God and with one another suffers greatly as a result. As the nineteenth-century Baptist preacher Charles Spurgeon said in his May 23, 1889, sermon "Charity and Purity," "Even in the pursuit of really good matters of policy, do you know any Christian man who goes into politics who is the better for it? If I find such a man, I will have him stuffed if I can, for I have never seen such a specimen yet. I will not say, do not attend to politics; but I do say, do not let politics stain you."[22]

Now, we realize that politics is somewhat of a necessary evil. We use the word *evil* because every politician is a sinner. Regardless of the political office an individual desires to hold or the political party with which they may or may not be affiliated, that individual is a sinner before they are elected to office, will be a sinner while they're in office, and will remain a sinner after they leave office. Again, Scripture provides the foundation for this assertion:

---

22 Charles H. Spurgeon, "2313. Charity And Purity," Answers in Genesis, September 26, 2017, https://answersingenesis.org/education/spurgeon-sermons/2313-charity-and-purity.

- "For all have sinned and fall short of the glory of God" (Romans 3:23).
- "Indeed, there is not a righteous man on earth who continually does good and who never sins" (Ecclesiastes 7:20).
- "The LORD has looked down from heaven upon the sons of men to see if there are any who understand, who seek after God. They have all turned aside, together they have become corrupt; there is no one who does good, not even one" (Psalm 14:2–3).

Despite the evidence of Scripture, some Christians still treat politicians as if the politicians can save them. Read carefully the warning that the prophet Samuel gave the people of Israel when they expressed the same feeling in their desire for a king:

> Then all the elders of Israel gathered together and came to Samuel at Ramah; and they said to him, "Behold, you have grown old, and your sons do not walk in your ways. Now appoint a king for us to judge us like all the nations." But the thing was displeasing in the sight of Samuel when they said, "Give us a king to judge us." And Samuel prayed to the LORD. The LORD said to Samuel, "Listen to the voice of the people in regard to all that they say to you, for they have not rejected you, but they have rejected Me from being king over them. Like all the deeds which they have done since the day that I brought them up from Egypt even to this day—in that they have forsaken Me and served other gods—so they are doing to you also. Now then, listen to their voice; however, you shall solemnly warn them and tell them of the procedure of the king who will reign over them."

> So Samuel spoke all the words of the LORD to the people who had asked of him a king. He said, "This will be the procedure of the king who will reign over you: he will take your sons and place them for himself in his chariots and among his horsemen and they will run before his chariots. He will appoint for himself commanders of thousands and of fifties, and some to do his plowing and to reap his harvest and to make his weapons of war and equipment for his chariots. He will also take your daughters for perfumers and cooks and bakers. He will take the best of your

fields and your vineyards and your olive groves and give them to his servants. He will take a tenth of your seed and of your vineyards and give to his officers and to his servants. He will also take your male servants and your female servants and your best young men and your donkeys and use them for his work. He will take a tenth of your flocks, and you yourselves will become his servants. Then you will cry out in that day because of your king whom you have chosen for yourselves, but the LORD will not answer you in that day."

Nevertheless, the people refused to listen to the voice of Samuel, and they said, "No, but there shall be a king over us, that we also may be like all the nations, that our king may judge us and go out before us and fight our battles."

Now after Samuel had heard all the words of the people, he repeated them in the LORD's hearing. The LORD said to Samuel, "Listen to their voice and appoint them a king." So Samuel said to the men of Israel, "Go every man to his city." (1 Samuel 8:4–22)

Sadly, what we witness in this text is similar to what we find Christians doing today. The people of Israel rejected God's rule for representative rule that allowed them less responsibility to God. They sought a king as savior rather than God as Lord and King. Even after Saul warned them of the pitfalls of having a king, they desired a king.

Yes, politicians are sinners. They make imperfect saviors at best. And yet, that universal reality neither negates nor nullifies our responsibility, as Christians, to remain faithful to God as it relates to our stewardship of and involvement in the political and electoral processes that place those sinful individuals in positions of authority over us.

Elections Are about Worldviews

For Christians, elections are actually less about issues and are more about worldviews. Regardless of the issue that happens to be of concern to us—whether it be abortion, taxes, school choice, or immigration—the stances and positions we take on those issues are the by-product of our worldview.

What exactly do we mean by the term *worldview*? Well, consider how Jeff Purswell, dean of Sovereign Grace Pastors College in Louisville, Kentucky, defines that term in the book *Worldliness: Resisting the Seduction of a Fallen World*:

> Before we examine how we're to relate to the world, we must understand it. We need a biblical worldview, a framework for understanding our human existence and environment that accords with reality. Whether we're aware of it or not, each of us has a set of beliefs and assumptions about ourselves and about the world we inhabit. Through the lens of these beliefs and assumptions—our worldview—we interpret our experiences, draw conclusions, and make decisions. Ultimately, our worldview determines how we live. That's why it's critical that these beliefs align with Scripture, for only there do we find God's take on our lives, on this world, indeed on reality itself. The Bible sets forth the contours of our existence, answering fundamental questions about our identity, our environment, our relationships, [and] our very purpose in life.[1]

Along the same lines of thought as Purswell, theologian Wayne Grudem, in *Politics According to the Bible*, writes,

> I believe that every Christian citizen who lives in a democracy has at the very least a minimal obligation to be well-informed and to vote for candidates and policies that are most consistent with biblical principles. The opportunity to help select the kind of government we will have is a stewardship that God entrusts to citizens in a democracy, a stewardship that we should not neglect or fail to appreciate. That at least means that Christians are responsible to learn enough about the important issues to be able to vote intelligently.[2]

The fuller context of the quote from Spurgeon's sermon "The Candle," which we cited above, is instructive at this point:

---

[1] Jeff Purswell, "How to Love the World," in *Worldliness: Resisting the Seduction of a Fallen World*, ed. C. J. Mahaney (Wheaton, IL: Crossway, 2017), 141.
[2] Wayne Grudem, *Politics According to the Bible: A Comprehensive Resource for Understanding Modern Political Issues in Light of Scripture* (Grand Rapids: Zondervan, 2010), 74.

> I long for the day when the precepts of the Christian religion shall be the rule among all classes of men, in all transactions. I often hear it said, "Do not bring religion into politics." This is precisely where it ought to be brought, and set there in the face of all men as on a candlestick. I would have the Cabinet and the members of Parliament do the work of the nation as before the Lord, and I would have the nation, either in making war or peace, consider the matter by the light of righteousness.[3]

What does this kind of "righteousness" look like? Where is this righteousness to be found so that we can apply it to our electoral decisions in a practical way? It is found, by both definition and example, in God and in his Word:

- "The words of the LORD are pure words; as silver tried in a furnace on the earth, refined seven times" (Psalm 12:6).

- "Make me know Your ways, O LORD; teach me Your paths. Lead me in Your truth and teach me, for You are the God of my salvation; for You I wait all the day" (Psalm 25:4–5).

- "Your word is a lamp to my feet and a light to my path" (Psalm 119:105).

- "Sanctify them in the truth; Your word is truth" (John 17:17).

- "For this reason we also constantly thank God that when you received the word of God which you heard from us, you accepted it not as the word of men, but for what it really is, the word of God, which also performs its work in you who believe" (1 Thessalonians 2:13).

- "All Scripture is inspired by God and profitable for teaching, for reproof, for correction, for training in righteousness, so that the man of God may be adequate, equipped for every good work" (2 Timothy 3:16–17).

---

3 Charles H. Spurgeon, "1594. The Candle," Answers in Genesis, December 8, 2014, https://answersingenesis.org/education/spurgeon-sermons/1594-the-candle.

- "For the word of God is living and active and sharper than any two-edged sword, and piercing as far as the division of soul and spirit, of both joints and marrow, and able to judge the thoughts and intentions of the heart" (Hebrews 4:12).

Scripture is clear that if we truly desire to know what the righteousness of God is and how to apply his righteousness in the decisions we make in every area of our lives so those decisions impact and influence the world around us in a godly way, we must go to God and to his Word. We cannot rely on our own subjective and fallible reasoning as it relates to how we are to view this fallen world and how we are to function and operate in it.

This is *worldview*, or how we view the world, and the lens by which we see things is critical to all the issues of life.

Worldview and the Founding Fathers

Whether we realize it or not, everyone has a worldview. For the believer, however, understanding a *biblical* worldview is primary. Secular culture has so embraced cultural Marxism that many have fallen prey to the historic revisionism of the *New York Times Magazine*'s 1619 Project. By their own admission, they are attempting to "reframe the country's history by placing the consequences of slavery and the contributions of black Americans at the very center of our national narrative."[4]

Understanding the worldview of the American founders is crucial to addressing the errors of projects like these. The idea that America was founded on slavery is incorrect. While the sin of slavery was a part of our history, the ideology (or worldview) possessed by many in America is what led to the abolition of slavery.

The worldview of our founders was biblically informed. Patrick Henry, the first governor of Virginia, who famously declared, "Give me

---

[4] "The 1619 Project," *The New York Times Magazine,* August 14, 2019, https://www.nytimes.com/interactive/2019/08/14/magazine/1619-america-slavery.html.

liberty or give me death," also had this to say regarding the worldview that established the United States: "It cannot be emphasized too often or too strongly that this great nation was founded not by religionists but by Christians; not on religions but on the gospel of Jesus Christ."[5]

Benjamin Franklin, at the age of eighty-one, spoke to the other delegates to the Constitutional Convention, saying, "In the contest with Britain, we had daily prayers in this room for Divine Protection. Our prayers, Sir, were heard and they were graciously answered. . . . Have we now forgotten this powerful friend? . . . I have lived Sir, a long time, and the longer I live the more convincing proofs I see of this truth: That God governs in the affairs of man. . . . I therefore move that prayers imploring the assistance of Heaven and its blessing on our deliberation, be held in this assembly every morning before we proceed to business."[6]

We share these quotes not to argue that all the founders were Christians but only to say that they held to a biblical worldview that informed how they led and the decisions they made.

This biblical worldview can likewise be seen everywhere within the founding documents of our nation. Dr. Paul T. Criss, in his article "Worldview and the U.S. Constitution," writes,

> The Constitution contains ideas that had never before been set forth in a previous government's documents. A full republic with checks and balances—a marvel among humankind. Where did they get these ideas? Political science professors at the University of Houston collected representative writings out of the founding era (1760–1805) and analyzed who they quoted to find out where they got their ideas. They collected fifteen thousand writings and identified 3,154 direct quotes of the founders; it took them ten years, but they took every quote back to its original source and discovered the top one hundred sources.

---

[5] Quoted in William Federer, comp., *America's God & Country: Encyclopedia of Quotations* (St. Louis: Amerisearch 2000), 289.
[6] Quoted in James Madison, *Notes of Debates in the Federal Convention of 1787* (NY: W.W. Morton & Co., Original 1787 reprinted 1987), 1:504, 421–51. John Eidsmoe, *Christianity and the Constitution – The Faith of Our Founding Fathers* (Grand Rapids: Baker Book House, 1993), 12–13, 208.

> They published their findings in a book called *The Origins of American Constitutionalism.* . . . The number one source cited was the Bible at 34%. Article 1, Section 8 about immigration compares with Leviticus 19:34. Article 2, Section 1 says the President must be a natural-born citizen from Deuteronomy 17:15 which says the head of your nation has to be born from among you. Article 3, Section 3 deals with witness for capital punishment for treason, but two people must testify to it in open court; this compares with Deuteronomy 17:6, [which] says you cannot be put to death unless it is established in the mouth of two to three witnesses. Article 3, Section 3 prohibits bills of attainder; Ezekiel 18:20 prohibits these in the Scripture. You can see the Bible throughout the Constitution, but because secularists never read the Bible, they are blind to these connections.[7]

The Founding Fathers, like all politicians and all mankind, were flawed, sinful men. The founding documents of our country were not inerrant or sufficient; had they been, there would be no need for amendments. But all that the founders engaged in and wrote was based on a worldview built on biblical principle, and as believers in Christ, the least we should do is emulate this same pattern.

Three Questions from Romans 13

Look back at the words of Charles Spurgeon's sermon "The Candle." He argues that believers in Christ are to view the issues of society and life "by the light of righteousness." Keeping that in mind, let's consider Romans 13 for a moment.

In Romans 13:4, the apostle Paul writes that government, the very concept of which is established by God (Romans 13:1), exists as "a minister of God to you for good." Now, that reality raises at least three questions for us as Christians, particularly as it relates to our responsibility as citizens in a democratic republic to participate in political and electoral processes. What does Paul mean that government is a "minister" for our good? What does "good" mean?

---

7 Dr. Paul T. Criss, "Worldview and the U.S. Constitution, Part 1," Adult Studies Faculty Resources (Belhaven University), September 17, 2018, http://blogs.belhaven.edu/asfaculty/2018/09/17/worldview-and-the-u-s-constitution-part-1.

And how is the good we're to derive from those who minster to us in government made effectual in society?

We want to address those questions one at a time.

A Minister of God

First, what does Paul mean when he says government exists as a "minister" of God to us for good?

The word "minister" is the Greek noun *diakonos*, from which the English word *deacon* is derived. In Romans 13:4, "minister" means "one who serves." More specifically, it means "one who executes the commands of another," especially those of a master. So, what Paul is saying in Romans 13:4 is that the men and women whom God sovereignly ordains (Romans 13:1) to serve in positions of authority within government are ultimately and primarily there to serve and obey him in those roles.

That reality is precisely why John Calvin, in his *Institutes of the Christian Religion*, says the following concerning those individuals:

> For to what high standards of probity, wisdom, mercy, sobriety and innocence must they hold themselves, when they realize that they have been ordained ministers of divine justice? How impudent would they be if they allowed the slightest iniquity access to their judgment seat, which they know to be the throne of the living God? How bold would they be if they pronounced unjust sentences with their lips, perceiving that they [their lips] are meant to be instruments of God's truth? With what conscience would they sign some wicked decree with the hand which, they know, ought to write God's own verdicts? In short, if they remember that they are deputies of God, they must make every effort and take every care in all they do to represent to men an image of God's providence, protection, goodness, mildness, and justice. This should indeed touch the hearts of our superiors, for it teaches them that they are like God's lieutenants, and that it is to him that they will have to account for the work which they have done. This word of admonition should rightly spur them on, for if they do something wrong, they injure not only those whom they afflict unfairly, but God as well, whose holy judgments they

defile (Isaiah 3:14–15). Again, they have abundant cause for consolation in reflecting that their calling is not profane or alien to a servant of God, but a most holy task, since the very work they do is God's.[8]

Calvin provides us with an exposition of what the role of minister should actually look like, which, accordingly, should influence us, as followers of Jesus Christ, to be spiritually discerning with regard to the men and women we choose to represent us in government.

In addition to Calvin's commentary, consider Article 36 of the Belgic Confession of Faith:

> We believe that our gracious God, because of the depravity of mankind, hath appointed kings, princes and magistrates, willing that the world should be governed by certain laws and policies; to the end that the dissoluteness of men might be restrained, and all things carried on among them with good order and decency. For this purpose he hath invested the magistracy with the sword, for the punishment of evil-doers, and for the protection of them that do well. And their office is, not only to have regard unto, and watch for the welfare of the civil state; but also that they protect the sacred ministry; and thus may remove and prevent all idolatry and false worship; that the kingdom of anti-Christ may be thus destroyed and the kingdom of Christ promoted. They must therefore countenance the preaching of the Word of the gospel everywhere, that God may be honored and worshipped by everyone, as He commanded in His Word.[9]

When we take together what John Calvin and the Belgic Confession are saying, we understand that those who represent us in government have a higher calling and purpose, one that has been established by God himself. If that's the case, every Christian voter should consider that he or she, too, has a higher calling than simply casting a vote for a specific candidate on the basis that that candidate happens to align with their perspective on a particular issue.

---

[8] John Calvin, *Institutes of the Christian Religion*, trans. Robert White (Edinburgh: Banner of Truth, 2014), 4.20.6.
[9] "Article 36: Of Magistrates," Belgic Confession of Faith, Protestant Reformed Churches in America (PRCA), March 18, 2013, http://www.prca.org/about/official-standards/creeds/three-forms-of-unity/belgic-confession/article-36.

Public Education: A Case Study

Consider the issue of public school education, for example. There is no argument that, in America today, public schools have essentially become indoctrination centers for promoting and exposing children to such unbiblical ideals as critical race theory (CRT) and the normalization of homosexuality and same-sex marriage. That is an unmitigated fact. With that in mind, believers would do well to consider these words of wisdom from the great Presbyterian theologian of Princeton Theological Seminary and, subsequently, of Westminster Theological Seminary, J. Gresham Machen, who, in his classic work, *Christianity & Liberalism*, says this:

> A public-school system, in itself, is indeed of enormous benefit to the [human] race. But it is of benefit only if it is kept healthy at every moment by the absolutely free possibility of the competition of private schools. A public-school system, if it means providing of free education for those who desire it, is a noteworthy and beneficent achievement of modern times; but when once it becomes monopolistic it is the most perfect instrument of tyranny which has yet been devised. Freedom of thought in the Middle Ages was combated by the Inquisition, but the modern method is far more effective. Place the lives of children in their formative years, despite the convictions of their parents, under the intimate control of experts appointed by the state, for them then to attend schools where the higher aspirations of humanity are crushed out, and where the mind is filled with the materialism of the day, and it is difficult to see how even the remnants of liberty can subsist. Such a tyranny, supported as it is by a perverse technique used as the instrument in destroying human souls, is certainly far more dangerous than the crude tyrannies of the past, which despite their weapons of fire and sword permitted thought at least to be free. The truth is that materialistic paternalism of the present day, if allowed to go on unchecked, will rapidly make of America one huge "Main Street," where spiritual adventure will be discouraged and democracy will be regarded as consisting in the reduction of all mankind to the proportions of the narrowest and least gifted of the citizens.[10]

---

10 J. Gresham Machen, *Christianity & Liberalism* (Glendale, CA: Bibliotech, 2019), 11–12.

Machen's words are important for Christian voters to consider, particularly as they relate to the education of our children, which begins in the home, not in the public school system. Not that we suggest, imply, or infer that homeschooling is a feasible alternative for every Christian family, nor is homeschooling to be an excuse to shield our children from the realities of a sinful world outside the home. Instead, we concur with the twentieth-century Presbyterian pastor and theologian Frances August Schaeffer, who said that "isolating the student from large sections of human knowledge is not the basis of a Christian education. Rather it is giving him or her the framework for total truth, rooted in the Creator's existence and in the Bible's teaching, so that in each step of the formal learning process the student will understand what is true and what is false and why it is true or false."[11]

The timeline of the formalization of education in the United States is fascinating. At the beginning, the process of education was primarily the responsibility of parents and the local church. The Puritans were the first to develop formal education in a classroom setting; however, this type of education was not focused on reading, writing, and arithmetic. The focus of the education was the development of moral character and citizenship through a growing understanding of the Word of God.

The first formal school in the United States was the Boston Latin School, established in 1635 in Boston, Massachusetts. It was a boys-only school established by Puritans and enrolled students in grades seven through twelve. This school only enrolled the best students as entrance was competitive.[12]

Compulsory education in the United States was a battle as the government began to believe there was benefit in equitable quality education in districts across the country. The State of New York in 1791 was the first state to codify compulsory education, mandating that all kids from five to eighteen years old would be in school. From

---

11 Francis A. Schaeffer, "Francis Schaeffer 'On Education,'" in "Priorities 1982," Francis Schaeffer Study Center, accessed June 18, 2021, http://www.schaefferstudycenter.org/francis-schaeffer-on-education.
12 "BLS History," Boston Latin School, accessed June 18, 2021, https://bls.org/apps/pages/index.jsp?uREC_ID=206116&type=d.

these small beginnings in local districts, the education movement grew to our current Federal Department of Education. Today, the national educational budget is $1.3 trillion dollars, and there are more than 56 million students enrolled in a variety of schools throughout the United States.[13]

There was a time when public schools could be trusted to educate our children apart from any overtly political agenda. But those days have long since passed. Humanism undergirds much of what our children are taught in public school today, with the goal of making them in the image of the teachers and professors who instruct them, replicating the worldview that those instructors themselves espouse.

As cultural apologist Dr. Peter Jones writes in his book *The Other Worldview: Exposing Christianity's Greatest Threat*,

> Humanism's respect for intelligence and rationality gave rise in Western culture to creative, independent thought that produced countless scientific and technological advances. Such progress laid the foundation for exploits as astounding as landing a man on the moon. However, independent human thought gradually came to be seen as the only norm for all truth—the ultimate source of all meaning. People began to conclude that belief in a world created by God and in things spiritual was merely superstitious, primitive myth to be abandoned as unthinking delusion. For the modern man, religion had to go.
>
> Thus, roughly between the 18th and 20th centuries, the Enlightenment, or Age of Reason, dominated the Western mind as the great opponent of Christianity. Only the ability of the human being, based no longer on faith in God but on faith in reason itself as the criteria of truth, would save us. A powerful optimism in the capacities of mankind to bring about a better world took the West by storm. Reason would replace primitive religious superstition and bring about the coming, glorious kingdom of man on earth.[14]

---

13 Melanie Hanson, "K-12 Enrollment & Student Population Statistics," EducationData.org, updated February 20, 2021, https://educationdata.org/k12-enrollment-statistics.
14 Peter Jones, *The Other Worldview: Exposing Christianity's Greatest Threat* (Bellingham, WA: Kirkdale, 2015), 18.

Not all public school systems are bad. But we would be both naïve and irresponsible as Christians to think there are not men and women in America running for political office at various levels of government who have their sights set on erasing from the hearts and minds of our young children every vestige of God, Jesus Christ, the Bible, and the gospel they have been taught in their homes and churches. As much as you may want to rear your children to be good little Christians, there are teachers, professors, and administrators in the public school system—at various levels—who want nothing more than to raise your children to be good little humanists.

To place this assertion into greater context, we want to quote from the book *Brainwashed: How Universities Indoctrinate America's Youth* by Ben Shapiro, who says this in chapter 7, titled "The War on God":

> The university system is the new city of Babel [Shapiro is citing Genesis 11]. Professors hope to build an intellectual tower that reaches into the heavens, to challenge God. They drag organized religion through the mud and then shoot arrows at its dirtied carcass. And once they've done that, they make moral judgments for all of mankind, as if obtaining a PhD conferred upon them some sort of supernatural moral wisdom. They wish to tear down biblical morality and place in its stead a morality of their own choosing. It is a degraded morality they seek to promote. Without God, there is no right and wrong, no good and bad. Anything goes. Life itself loses value, and with that loss of value comes a loss of societal strength. In short, America becomes France. What these professors want is a jihad against God, a crusade against traditional morality. And their battlefields are lecture halls full of innocent civilians.[15]

A Minister for Good

We want to continue our examination of the apostle Paul's words in Romans 13:4 by addressing the second of the three questions posed earlier: What does Paul mean when he says government is "a minister of God to you for good"? What does that word *good* actually mean, and how are we to understand it in the context of elections?

---

15   Ben Shapiro, *Brainwashed: How Universities Indoctrinate America's Youth* (Nashville: WND, 2004), 133–134.

The word *good* in Romans 13:4 is the Greek adjective *agathos*, which denotes that which is perfect, distinguished, and excellent in every respect. The word *agathos* is the same Greek used in Romans 12:2, "And do not be conformed to this world, but be transformed by the renewing of your mind, so that you may prove what the will of God is, that which is good [*agathos*] and acceptable and perfect."

If government exists as a minister, as a *diakonos*, a servant of God to us for good, it stands to reason that professing Christians who are planning to vote, regardless of the office, should endeavor to support candidates who are committed to using their God-given, God-ordained position and power in government to bring about in society the kind of *agathos*, the kind of good, that is acceptable and perfect as God defines it.

Why is that important? Because politicians are sinners too, and so are the people they govern, so we need to be circumspect and judicious in deciding how our votes are cast. We say this against the backdrop of what the nineteenth-century American historian and educator Emma Hart Willard said in the year 1843: "The government of the United States is acknowledged by the wise and good of other nations, to be the most free, impartial, and righteous government of the world; but all agree, that for such a government to be sustained for many years, the principles of truth and righteousness, taught in the Holy Scriptures, must be practiced. The rulers must govern in the fear of God, and the people obey the laws."[16]

Willard's statement, especially the last sentence where she emphasized that a righteous government is one wherein "the rulers must govern in the fear of God" and "the people obey the laws," brings to mind the words of twentieth-century Welsh theologian and preacher D. Martyn Lloyd-Jones, who, in his commentary on Romans 13, says this:

> It is only Christians who see the real need for the state. It is Christians alone who really believe in sin, who know what sin is, and the power it has in each person's life. They realize, as nobody

---

16 Emma Willard, in "The Washington Flyer," December 10, 2010, http://www.aacs.org/assets/Washington-Flyer/2010/WF121010rev.pdf.

else can, the extent to which sin can lead us, both individually and collectively. They also see more clearly than anyone else the necessity for controlling sin and its manifestations and results. That is why Christians should always be on the side of law and order. Humanists do not believe in sin at all, so they do not see the same need for legislation, and you will therefore find that, as a general rule, they are opposed to various laws. But not only do Christians see the need for law, control, and order, they know that God Himself has made this provision for the maintenance of life. Try to think what life in the world would be like if you suddenly banished all the laws; if you banished the police force and everything that is designed [by God] to preserve law and order.[17]

And we know that today many individuals and organizations in America have absolutely no respect for law and order, who want to defund entire police departments, and who use fear, intimidation, anarchy, and violence (all in the name of "justice" and "equality") to bring about the kind of humanistic, anti-God society they desire.

Law and Order: An Example of Good

The issue of law and order is of fundamental importance to many professing Christians. Law and order is a universal issue. There is no culture or society on this planet that doesn't subscribe to some construct of law and order. We know from 1 Corinthians 14:33 that "God is not a God of confusion but of peace." When you really think about it, laws exist to protect us from one another. Or, to put it differently, to protect sinners from other sinners.

Irving Kristol, an American journalist known as the father of neoconservatism, argued in an essay forty-five years ago that republican virtue is fundamentally the virtue of public-spiritedness as the Founding Fathers knew it: "Public spiritedness means curbing one's passions and moderating one's opinions in order to achieve a large consensus that will ensure domestic tranquility. We think of public-spiritedness as a form of self-expression, an exercise

---

17 D. Martyn Lloyd-Jones, *Exposition of Romans 13: Life in Two Kingdoms* (London: Banner of Truth, 1973), 51.

in self-righteousness. The Founders thought of it as a form of self-control, an exercise in self-government."[18]

For followers of Christ, the question becomes "What is your theology of law and order?" Is it based in the objective truth of Scripture? Or is it shaped by the subjective and changeable constructs of the world? In posing these questions, we're reminded of the words of pastor and theologian A. W. Tozer, who, in his book *Culture: Living as Citizens of Heaven on Earth*, says this:

> As a church we must . . . embody in a supreme degree the purposes for which we exist. There are three purposes for which we exist on earth: to worship, to witness, and to work. When people are converted [to Christ] they immediately change their citizenships. They are no longer citizens of earth except in a provisory way. They are now citizens of heaven. Christians, when they are born of God, immediately shift their citizenships and become pilgrims and strangers where they used to be citizens. All who are born anew have new natures. God becomes our Father and Jesus becomes our Brother, we become the habitation of the Spirit and heaven is our fatherland. Why then are we left here on earth among strangers? We are left here to worship, to witness, and to work. Those three things are what we are here for.[19]

Effectual Good

Returning to Romans 13:4, let's consider the final of the three questions posed earlier in this chapter. How is the "good" that we're to derive from those who minister to us in government made effectual in society? We know there are professing believers, perhaps some reading this chapter, who are of the opinion that Christians should not be involved in political processes at all, that our primary concern and obligation is for God's church and for meeting the needs of God's people. With all due respect to those who may be of that conviction,

---

18 Irving Kristol, "Republican Virtue vs. Servile Institutions," Contemporary Thinkers, March 21, 2014, https://contemporarythinkers.org/irving-kristol/essay/republican-virtue-vs-servile-institutions.
19 A. W. Tozer, *Culture: Living as Citizens of Heaven on Earth* (Chicago: Moody, 2016) 66–67.

listen to this argument from the book *Practical Religion* by nineteenth-century Anglican theologian J. C. Ryle:

> True believers are always represented as mixing in the world, doing their duty in it, and glorifying God by patience, meekness, purity, and courage in their several positions, and not by cowardly desertion of them. Moreover, it is foolish to suppose that we can keep the world and the devil out of our hearts by going into holes and corners. True religion and unworldliness are best seen, not in timidly forsaking the post which God has allotted to us, but in manfully standing our ground, and showing the power of grace to overcome evil.[20]

What Ryle is saying there is that while we are in this world, the best way for Christians to effectuate gospel-centered influence in the world is to be what Jesus described metaphorically in the Sermon on the Mount as "salt" and "light" (Matthew 5:13–16). And one way we can do that is by being involved in the electoral process and to do what we can, as God gives us wisdom and discernment, to support godly policies and help elect men and women to office who embrace those godly policies toward the larger goal of "showing the power of grace to overcome evil."

We believe the issue of abortion is a prime example of how believers in Christ can put J. C. Ryle's counsel into action in a very practical way, particularly as we consider that third question, how is the "good" we're to derive from those who minister to us in government made effectual in society? Abortion, however, is a divisive issue, even among professing Christians. For many professing Christians, abortion is *the* singular issue on which they determine their vote. So, we direct your attention to the following words from Dr. John P. Stead, who, in the book *Think Biblically: Recovering a Christian Worldview*, says:

> Evangelicals should reject becoming involved in a contest for control of political institutions because this is the modus operandi of modern authoritarianism and totalitarianism. It is only a short step from the control of governmental institutions to the control

---

20 J. C. Ryle, *Practical Religion* (Darlington, United Kingdom: Evangelical Press, 2001), 275.

of not only people's public lives, but also their private lives. This control would occur even if done in the name of Christ.

Christians should reject the temptation to seek political power for its own sake in view of the pervasiveness of a believer's sin capacity. Will "godly Christians" consistently make biblical decisions concerning morality and social justice? That this has occurred only infrequently through the history of western civilization testifies to the questionable validity of this belief. Christians cannot agree on many moral and social issues, let alone on how governmental institutions should be used. Believers need to be reminded that there can be no healthy or lasting change of social structures without a redemptive change in people, which is why Christ came [more than] two thousand years ago.

What America needs more than anything else is an evangelizing church exercising the power of the Cross to change people's lives. As people whose primary citizenship is in heaven and as members of Christ's kingdom, we are confronted by a world system concerned with gaining political power. The church must reject the temptation to control political institutions, while seeking locally to alter the lives of those around it. By their speech and lives, Christians must show men and women that there is only one way to have a right relationship with God, the way of the Cross. Believers in Christ need to stand in every way—spiritually, intellectually, morally, and politically—as the vital, separated alternative to a world system that glories in materialism, self-indulgence, and political power.[21]

A Kingdom Not of this World

The subject matter we're dealing with in this chapter is a good opportunity to remind ourselves of Jesus's words in John 18:36, where he declares to Pilate, "My kingdom is not of this world." Many of us are familiar with this verse but too often take it too lightly.

The word "kingdom" in John 18:36 is the Greek noun *basileia*. In his commentary on John 18:36, the eighteenth-century Bible expositor

---

[21] John P. Stead, "Developing a Biblical View of Church and State," in *Think Biblically: Recovering a Christian Worldview*, ed. John MacArthur (Wheaton, IL: Crossway, 2003) 293, 295.

and commentator Matthew Henry provides some hermeneutical clarity on what Jesus meant when He said to Pilate, "My kingdom is not of this world":

> Christ gave an account of the nature of his kingdom. Its nature is not worldly; it is a kingdom within men, set up in their hearts and consciences; its riches spiritual, its power spiritual, and it glory within. Its supports are not worldly; its weapons are spiritual; it needed not, nor used, force to maintain and advance it, nor opposed any kingdom but that of sin and Satan. Its object and design are not worldly. When Christ said, I am the Truth, he said, in effect, I am a King. He conquers by the convincing evidence of truth; he rules by the commanding power of truth. The subjects of this kingdom are those that are of the truth.[22]

Our point is this: politics, at its most fundamental level, is the business of kingdom building. Politics is about building earthly kingdoms and legacies whose foundations are constructed on sinking sand. And as much as we should desire that truly godly men and women "minister" to us in government (Romans 13:4), as Christians, we are neither to view nor use politics or elections as a means or vehicle to engage in kingdom building here on earth. It is crucial that we understand that. Regardless of what issues we happen to be most concerned with or most passionate about, the immutable truth remains that this world and its lusts are passing away (1 John 2:17). That reality should point us back to what the Scriptures declare to us in such passages as these:

- "But according to His promise we are looking for new heavens and a new earth, in which righteousness dwells" (2 Peter 3:13).
- "Do not work for the food which perishes, but for the food which endures to eternal life, which the Son of Man will give to you" (John 6:27).
- "It is better to take refuge in the LORD than to trust in man. It is better to take refuge in the LORD than to trust in princes" (Psalm 118:8–9).

---

22 Matthew Henry, *The New Matthew Henry Commentary*, ed. Martin H. Manser (Grand Rapids: Zondervan, 2010) 1851–1852.

- "Do not trust in princes, in mortal man, in whom there is no salvation" (Psalm 146:3).

If we are honest, we will admit that some professing Christians view politics as salvific. They are of the belief that if Christians would just band together and vote either for or against this candidate or that candidate, it will somehow result in our society becoming more righteous.

The Greek philosopher Solon, regarded as one of the "seven wise men" of Greece, said, "Society is well governed when its people obey the magistrates, and the magistrates obey the law."[23] But we must remember what we previously said—politicians are sinners before they're elected to office and remain sinners while they're in office. No matter how polished or articulate they may appear on the outside, the words of Ecclesiastes 7:20 apply to them as well as to anyone else: "Indeed, there is not a righteous man on earth who continually does good and who never sins." We must not place a level of trust in any political candidate that is above and beyond what their inherently sinful natures make them capable of.

This is no new revelation, as again, those men whose biblically informed worldview crafted the shape of our nation observed:

- "Despotism may govern without faith, but liberty cannot. Religion is much more necessary in the republic . . . than in the monarchy. . . . How is it possible that society should escape destruction if the moral tie is not strengthened in proportion as the political tie is relaxed? And what can be done with a people who are their own masters if they are not submissive to the Deity?" (Alexis de Tocqueville).[24]
- "We have been assured, sir, in the sacred writings, that 'except the Lord build the house they labor in vain that build it.' I firmly believe this; and I also believe that without His concurring aid we shall succeed in this political building

---

23 Solon, quoted in *A Dictionary of Thoughts,* ed. Tryon Edwards (Detroit: F.B. Dickerson, 1908), 204.
24 Alexis de Tocqueville, *Democracy in America* (Italy: Vintage Books, 1990) 1:318.

no better than the builders of Babel; we shall be divided by our little partial, local interests, our projects will be confounded and we ourselves shall become a reproach and a byword down to future ages. And, what is worse, mankind may hereafter, from this unfortunate instance, despair of establishing government by human wisdom and leave it to chance, war, or conquest" (Benjamin Franklin).[25]

- "Can the liberties of a nation be thought secure when we have removed their only firm basis, a conviction in the minds of the people that these liberties are of the gift of God? That they are not to be violated but with his wrath?" (Thomas Jefferson).[26]

How Then Shall We Vote?

Given all that has been said to this point, a question each of us who names the name of Jesus Christ must consider is this: What is your motive when you go out to vote? What is the impetus that inspires you to vote the way you do? Is it your own self-centered desires and concerns? Or is it the gospel of Jesus Christ and a desire to see his righteousness reflected through those who, by God's sovereign will, have been ordained by God to "minister" to us for our good?

When we look at an election in that light, how we cast our vote becomes something every professing Christian should think very seriously and circumspectly about. It is indeed a weighty proposition when we stop to think that God will hold each of us accountable not only for how we cast our votes but also for the motives involved in casting our votes the way we did (Romans 14:12).

As we consider seriously our role as Christians and citizens, we must remember again that politics is not salvific. Saviors are not elected. Politicians cannot save you. There is but one Savior of the world (Acts 4:12), and he is never up for re-election.

---

25 Benjamin Franklin, Our Republic, accessed June 18, 2021, https://www.ourrepubliconline.com/Quote/42.
26 Thomas Jefferson, "*Notes on Virginia*, ME 2:227. 1782," Our Republic, accessed June 18, 2021, https://www.ourrepubliconline.com/Quote/307.

Let the words of Psalm 146:3 resonate in your mind again as any election day approaches: "Do not trust in princes, in mortal man, in whom there is no salvation." The word "trust" in Psalm 146:3 means "to find security and to set one's hope and confidence in."

This means we must not place our confidence and trust even in those politicians who profess to be followers of Christ, because they are fallible as well. To quote Spurgeon from his sermon "Hideous Discovery," "sin is not a splash of mud upon man's exterior, it is a filth generated within himself."[27] Renowned English Puritan of the seventeenth century John Owen, in his book *Indwelling Sin in Believers*, said, "The one who understands the evil of his own heart is the only useful, fruitful, solid believer. Others are fit only to delude themselves, and to disquiet families, churches, and every association."[28]

Followers of Jesus Christ are to place their confidence and trust in Christ and in him alone. Toward that end, let us strive to follow the example of the psalmist in Psalm 31:14–15, who said, "But as for me, I trust in You, O Lord, I say, 'You are my God.' My times are in Your hand."

One last time we remind you of what Spurgeon said, that we are to regard the issues and individuals with whom we are confronted in the political realm "by the light of righteousness." We are not to regard them by the light of emotions, feelings, circumstances, or political expediency, traditions, or loyalties.

It is this very thing that often gets us in trouble when it comes to politics. We look to politicians and to the government to say yes to what God has already said no to. We don't want to be told no by God, so what do we do? We deliberately search for ways to circumvent and ignore the loving and protective boundaries God has established for us. We want to be our own god and live our lives in complete autonomy. And one of the ways we do that is by electing men and

---

27 Charles H. Spurgeon, "1911. Hideous Discovery," Answers in Genesis, March 11, 2016, https://answersingenesis.org/education/spurgeon-sermons/1911-hideous-discovery.
28 John Owen, *The Indwelling Sin in Believers* (Dallas: Gideon House Books, 2015), 4.

women to political office who will help us fulfill that sinful desire to be our own god. The result of this is what we see in our culture today. Same-sex marriage is now legal. It is legal to murder unborn image-bearers of God. Homosexuality, lesbianism, and transgenderism are now protected behaviors. All this and more because we refuse to submit ourselves to the boundaries God has established.

Minds Trained on Christ

In Colossians 3:2, the apostle exhorts believers to "set your mind on the things above, not on the things that are on earth." With that challenge in mind, we close with these words from the book *The Loveliness of Christ* by the Puritan theologian Samuel Rutherford as an encouragement to keep our hearts and minds trained on Jesus Christ and to not put our faith or trust in the mutable promises of fallible politicians:

> I urge upon you ... a nearer communion with Christ and a growing communion. There are curtains to be drawn by in Christ that we [have never seen], and new foldings of love in Him. ... There are so many plies [folds] in it; therefore dig deep, and sweat, and labour, and take pains for Him, and set [aside] so much time in the day for Him as you can: He will be won with labour. ... My counsel is that ye come out and leave the multitude and let Christ have your company. Let them take clay and this present world who love it: Christ is a more worthy and noble portion: blessed are those who get Him.[29]

Questions for Discussion

1. In this chapter, what are the key verses used to establish a proper mindset about our participation in elections?
2. Why is it important to have a proper soteriology and Christology when engaging in the political process?
3. What do we mean when we say, "Elections are about worldview"?

---

[29] Samuel Rutherford, *The Loveliness of Christ* (Carlisle, PA: Banner of Truth, 2007), 16, 56.

4. From the reading, how did you respond to the three questions in Romans 13?
5. How should a Christian approach voting?

About the Authors

Darrell B. Harrison serves as Dean of Social Media at Grace to You, the media ministry of John MacArthur, located in Valencia, California. Darrell is the cohost of the Just Thinking podcast, one of the leading Christian podcasts in America. He is a Fellow of the Black Theology and Leadership Institute (BTLI) at Princeton Theological Seminary and holds a C:TM from Princeton Theological Seminary. Darrell and his wife, Melissa, reside in Valencia, California.

Virgil L. Walker serves as the Executive Director of Operations for G3 Ministries with Founder and President, Joshua Buice. Virgil is the cohost of the Just Thinking podcast. Virgil completed his Master of Business Administration (MBA), is a Fellow of The Freedom Center, and serves on the Steering Committee for the Conservative Baptist Network (CBN). Virgil and his wife, Tomeka, have three children.

Scripture Index

Old Testament

Genesis

1	23, 141
1:26–28	141
1:27	11, 45, 93, 134, 143, 146, 152, 153
1:27–28	45, 48
2:15	51
2:15–17	141
2:16–17	15
3	24, 78, 94, 144
3:16	69
4	24
5:2	11
6:5	24, 81
11	171

Exodus

18:15–26	24
20:9–10	51
20:15	38, 43, 63
20:17	43

Exodus (cont)

35	17
35:5	17
35:21–22	17
35:26	17
35:29	17
36	17
36:2	18

Leviticus

5:1–6	129
18:21	87
19:15	12, 17, 96
19:34	165

Deuteronomy

1:17	96
8:2–3	14
10:17	12

Deuteronomy (cont)	
15:11	70
16:19	19
17:6	165
17:15	165
24:16	126, 138

1 Samuel	
8:4–22	160
12:19–21	99

Job	
21:14	78

Psalms	
12:6	162
14:2–3	159
15:1–4	98
15:4	16
19:1	141
25:4–5	162
31:14–15	180
34:10	8
84:11	9
103:12	126
103:19	15, 23, 25
115:3	23
118:8–9	72, 177
119:105	162
121	9
124:8	8
130:3	127
135:6	23
146:3	178, 180
146:3–4	72

Proverbs	
5:21–23	41
12:22	16
14:23	39
14:23–24	51
16:4	23
19:15	39
19:21	23
22:2	48
22:29	51
28:19	51
28:21	96

Ecclesiastes	
1:9	33
5:8	71
7:20	81, 159, 178
9:3	74, 81, 144

Isaiah	
3:14–15	167
64:6	67
65:17	60

Jeremiah	
17:9	110, 154

Ezekiel	
18:19–22	127, 138
18:20	165
18:22	127

New Testament

Matthew

1:21	70
5:11–12	4
5:13–16	86, 175
5:45	15
6:19–21	54
6:30–33	8
11:28	22
16:27	23
26:11	68

Mark

1:15	70

Luke

3:12–13	133
4:18	71
19:1–8	132
19:2	132
19:7	133
19:8	133
20:21	13

John

1:12–13	107
3:17–18	56
3:19–20	143
3:27	68
6:27	21, 177
6:33–34	21
17:3	50

John (cont)

17:17	67, 162
18:36	69, 176
19:1–7	131

Acts

4:12	179
10:34–35	13

Romans

1	82, 83
1:18	144
1:18–19	82
1:18–20	140
1:20	82
2:11	13
3:23	159
5:12	80
8	70
8:6–8	143
8:19–21	20
8:22	69
8:32	22
10:9–10	43
11:36	23
12:2	113, 172
13	11, 23, 39
13:1	23, 165, 166
13:1–5	24
13:4	22, 165, 166, 171, 172, 174, 177
13:8	16
14:12	130, 179

1 Corinthians

2:12–14	81
6:19–20	86
14:33	173
15:3	158

2 Corinthians

5:14	43
9:7	39
10:5	3

Galatians

1:8	31
1:8–9	64
6:7	15, 98
6:9–10	43
6:10	20, 68

Ephesians

4:11–14	111
4:28	38, 56

Philippians

2:3–4	79
2:13	23
4:6, 19	99
4:19	8

Colossians

1:16	23
2:13–14	126
3:1–3.	158
3:2	181

1 Thessalonians

2:13	162

2 Thessalonians

2:11–12	143
3:6–12	54
3:7–12	37, 38
3:10	15, 54

1 Timothy

5:3	40
5:16	40
5:21	95
6:8	21

2 Timothy

3:16–17	162

Hebrews

4:12	163

James

2:8	13
2:8–9	13
3:13–16	75
3:13–18	85

1 Peter

3:15	155

2 Peter

3:13	22, 60, 71, 72, 177

1 John

2:2	128
2:9-11	136
2:15–17	22, 158
2:17	177
3:4	24+
4:20	136

Revelation

22:11	71

Other Titles from Founders Press

BY WHAT STANDARD? God's World... God's Rules.
Edited by Jared Longshore

> I'm grateful for the courage of these men and the clarity of their voices. This is a vitally important volume, sounding all the right notes of passion, warning, instruction, and hope.
>
> —Phil Johnson, Executive Director,
> Grace To You

Truth & Grace Memory Books
Edited by Thomas K. Ascol

> Memorizing a good, age-appropriate catechism is as valuable for learning the Bible as memorizing multiplication tables is for learning mathematics.
>
> —Dr. Don Whitney, Professor,
> The Southern Baptist Theological Seminary

Dear Timothy: Letters on Pastoral Ministry
Edited by Thomas K. Ascol

> Get this book. So many experienced pastors have written in this book it is a gold mine of wisdom for young pastors in how to preach and carry out their ministerial life.
>
> —Joel Beeke, President,
> Puritan Reformed Theological Seminary

The Mystery of Christ, His Covenant & His Kingdom
By Samuel Renihan

> This book serves for an excellent and rich primer on covenant theology and demonstrates how it leads from the Covenant of Redemption to the final claiming and purifying of the people given by the Father to the Son.
>
> —Tom Nettles, Retired Professor of Historical Theology,
> The Southern Baptist Theological Seminary

***Strong And Courageous:** Following Jesus Amid the Rise of America's New Religion*
By Tom Ascol and Jared Longshore

> We have had quite enough of "Be Nice and Inoffensive." We are overflowing with "Be Tolerant and Sensitive." It is high time that we were admonished to "Be Strong and Courageous."'
>
> —Jim Scott Orrick, Author, Pastor of Bullitt Lick Baptist Church

Additional titles

Wisdom for Kings & Queens: Truth for Life from the Book of Proverbs
By Jared Longshore

Still Confessing: An Exposition of the Baptist Faith & Message 2000
By Daniel Scheiderer

By His Grace and for His Glory
By Tom Nettles

Getting the Garden Right
By Richard C. Barcellos

The Law and the Gospel
By Ernie Reisinger

Traditional Theology & the SBC
By Tom Ascol

Teaching Truth, Training Hearts
By Tom Nettles

Coming in 2021

Praise Is His Gracious Choice:
Corporate Worship Expressing Biblical Truth
By Dr. Tom Nettles

The Transcultural Gospel
By E.D. Burns

Ancient Gospel, Brave New World
By E.D. Burns

Galatians: He Did It All
By Baruch Maoz

Missions by the Book
By Chad Vegas and Alex Kocman

Baptist Symbolics Vol. 1
For the Vindication of the Truth: A Brief Exposition of the
First London Baptist Confession of Faith
By James M. Renihan

Order these titles and more at press.founders.org